SRA
Read to Achieve

Comprehending Content-Area Text

Professional Development Guide

Nancy Marchand-Martella

Ronald Martella

McGraw Hill SRA

Columbus, OH

Acknowledgments

From Hasbrouck, J., & Tindal, G. (2006, April). Oral reading fluency norms: A valuable assessment tool for reading teachers. THE READING TEACHER, 59(7), 636–644. Copyright 2006 by the International Reading Association. Used with permission.

The authors thank the following educators and their students for conducting field tests of materials for this program:

- Mary Driscoll, Prairie View Elementary, Mead School District, Spokane, Washington

- Angie Wittwer, Evergreen Elementary, Mead School District, Spokane, Washington

- Charlene Stringham, Tulare City Schools, Tulare, California

- Terry Dodds, W.C. Cupe Middle School, Columbus, Ohio

- Anne-Marie Ophus and Erin Honeycutt, Freeman High School, Freeman, Washington

- Nadine Parrish-Parker, Sprague and Lamont School District, Sprague, Washington

The authors appreciate the assistance of Lisa Warner and Angela Przychodzin in the writing of lessons and Bethany Leonard and Holly Latterell in the development of materials for this program.

Photo Credits

Cover photo © Carl Zapp

SRAonline.com
SRADirectInstruction.com

Printed in the United States of America.

Send all inquiries to this address:
SRA/McGraw-Hill
4400 Easton Commons
Columbus, OH 43219

ISBN: 978-0-07-621994-0
MHID: 0-07-621994-1

6 7 8 9 CCI 13 12 11

About the Authors

Nancy Marchand-Martella, Ph.D.

Dr. Nancy Marchand-Martella is a professor in the Department of Counseling, Developmental, and Educational Psychology at Eastern Washington University, where she teaches classes in academic remediation with a focus on reading, writing, spelling, and math interventions. Dr. Marchand-Martella has more than twenty-five years of experience working with at-risk populations. She provides technical assistance to numerous states as part of Reading First and Basic Tutorial Credentialing initiatives. Dr. Marchand-Martella has been published in 123 publications, including five textbooks, ten chapters/ contributions or manuals, seventy-six refereed journal articles, and twenty-four book reviews/reports/nonrefereed articles/instructional products. Most of Dr. Marchand-Martella's research has been conducted in intermediate and secondary settings. She is an author of a two-level vocabulary program and is also an SRA/McGraw-Hill author of the six-level *SRA Lesson Connections* program that's used with *Reading Mastery Signature Edition*. She has made 228 professional presentations, including 137 national/international workshops, keynotes, and formal presentations on effective instruction. Dr. Marchand-Martella has also presented at ninety-one regional/state workshops on effective instruction. She worked several years as a *Corrective Reading* trainer, serves as the editor of the *Journal of Direct Instruction,* and is a review board member of three peer-reviewed journals. Dr. Marchand-Martella has reviewed core, supplemental, and reading intervention programs for K–3 and 4–12 state reading panels and serves on the K–12 reading advisory panel for higher education in the state of Washington.

Ronald Martella, Ph.D.

Dr. Ronald Martella is a professor in the Department of Counseling, Developmental, and Educational Psychology at Eastern Washington University, where he teaches classes in behavior management and research methodology. Dr. Martella has more than twenty-five years of experience working with at-risk populations. He provides technical assistance to numerous states and districts for positive behavior support (PBS)/behavior management for students with or without disabilities. Dr. Martella has been published in 114 publications, including five textbooks, ten chapters/contributions or manuals, seventy-two refereed journal articles, and twenty-one book reviews/nonrefereed articles/instructional products. Most of Dr. Martella's research has been conducted in intermediate and secondary settings. He is an SRA/McGraw-Hill author of the six-level *SRA Lesson Connections* program that's used with *Reading Mastery Signature Edition* and has made 143 professional presentations, including seventy-five national/international workshops and sixty-eight regional/state workshops on behavior management, effective instruction, or research methodology. Dr. Martella serves on the editorial board of three peer-reviewed journals.

Contents

Contents

Overview

Purpose

SRA Read to Achieve: Comprehending Content-Area Text is an explicit reading-for-understanding program for students in grades 6–12. **Read to Achieve** teaches important skills and strategies needed for students to be successful in content-area classes. Students learn to read their textbooks and other informational text more effectively, to take notes from these materials as well as during classroom lectures, and to study their notes for better performance on classroom assessments. Rather than *teaching* content, **Read to Achieve** teaches students how to *access* content at higher levels. Unfortunately, the challenge of accessing information from science and social studies text and lectures can be a daunting task for most students. **Read to Achieve** makes learning these skills and strategies less daunting and more enjoyable. Students participate in collaborative learning and "Beyond the Book" activities throughout the program.

Read to Achieve is built using a solid differentiated-instruction framework. By using differentiated instruction, you can provide students with more or less instruction and practice based on their unique needs. (**NOTE:** If you have doubts about a student's entry-level skills, administer the reproducible **SRA Read to Achieve: Comprehending Content-Area Text** Placement Test, located in Appendix B of this guide.) Students can participate in **Read to Achieve** if they have learned to decode fluently but haven't mastered the comprehension, vocabulary, and fluency skills and strategies needed to read content-area text with ease and better understanding. In **Read to Achieve,** students learn important foundational skills for present and future learning environments, where more difficult, expository-based materials are commonplace (middle school, high school, and college).

Features

The **Read to Achieve** program is built using a solid research base, including studies about explicit teaching, adolescent literacy, and content-area literature. Features of the program are listed below.

- All details of the program are designed to provide **differentiated instruction** to learners. The instructional sequence progresses from strong teacher support to student independence, allowing you to provide as much of the program as your students need. (Again, if in doubt about the entry-level skills of a particular learner, individually administer the Placement Test.) Additionally, beginning in Unit 2, unit assessments are administered on a weekly basis to ensure student success. These assessments provide differentiated-instruction criteria and strategies to promote student mastery; the assessments also contain specific recommendations for students approaching mastery, students at mastery, and English-Language Learners (ELL).

- The program can be used as an effective part of a **three-tier reading model.** As such, **Read to Achieve** may be used as a supplement to your core program or

as part of your strategic or intensive intervention efforts.

- Lessons are arranged in **units**, much like the units found in many content-area textbooks. Units in the student Content Reader contain lessons about both science and social studies topics. Science topics include living things, ecosystems, and the atmosphere, while social studies topics include the Roman Empire, the Panama Canal, and the American Revolution. Daily lessons typically can be presented in one class period (forty-five to fifty minutes).

- *Read to Achieve* is based on **cumulative skill development** and matches grade-level and Lexile Framework® recommendations for adolescent readers. Lexile levels in *Read to Achieve* are 700L–900L for Units 1–6, 800L–1000L for Units 7–12, and 900L–1100L for Units 13–20. Teacher-selected science and social studies textbooks are used in Units 21–25.

- All skills and strategies are taught through **explicit instruction** embedded in content-area text. Explicit instruction provides clear, no-nonsense directions for teachers, thus eliminating the guesswork on how to teach content-area skills and strategies. Further, explicit instruction includes teacher think-alouds and guided- and independent-practice opportunities to maximize student success.

- **Text-based collaborative learning** is evident in *Read to Achieve.* As students complete activities, they interact with one another in most aspects of the program. Activities such as "think-pair-share," which contain the wording *Work with your partner to . . . ,* encourage student collaboration and motivation to complete program activities.

- An emphasis is placed on **decoding multipart words,** in which students learn to read longer and more difficult words before determining their meanings. Decoding multipart words involves

breaking words into smaller parts so the words can be read more easily—without using formal syllabication. When teaching formal syllabication, teachers show students how to break a word into syllables—rather than parts—according to conventions used in dictionaries; the teacher then must teach students syllable types. *Read to Achieve* teaches students to break words into smaller parts (not syllables) so each part has one vowel sound, thereby decreasing the complexity of the strategy. Syllable types are not taught.

- The program's focus is **reading to learn.** Students spend their time immersed in comprehension, vocabulary, and fluency-building activities. These activities are conducted to facilitate student access to content-area materials and other diverse texts.

- *Read to Achieve* teaches **real-world strategies** such as how to (a) take notes from a textbook, (b) figure out what difficult words mean, (c) take lecture notes, and (d) research questions of interest. All levels of Bloom's Taxonomy are woven into activities, and higher-order thinking skills are promoted. Metacognitive strategies teach "thinking about thinking" and critical problem-solving skills.

- **Formative assessment** is conducted. Students complete Workbook and notepaper-based activities, unit assessments, standardized-test practice, and fluency checks on a frequent basis to inform instructional practices. Fluency goal lines equivalent to the fiftieth, seventy-fifth, and ninetieth percentiles for middle school were used as noted by Hasbrouck and Tindal's 2006 oral-reading fluency norm data.

- The goal of *Read to Achieve* is **generalization.** Skills and strategies are taught and folded into more complex strategies for maximum use. Ultimately, the Workbook and Content Reader are faded to ensure student transfer. In later units, Strategy Bookmarks take the place of graphic organizers, and students use notebook paper and their own classroom science and social studies textbooks. The program also contains other generalization exercises, such as "Beyond the Book" extension activities centered on various types of informational text (magazine articles, Web sites, students' classroom science and social studies textbooks, and so on). Through these carefully crafted program elements, self-directed learning and transfer are promoted. The key is to ensure student success *beyond* the program.

> In later units, Strategy Bookmarks take the place of graphic organizers.

Materials

Teacher Materials

Teacher materials for *Read to Achieve* consist of the following:

- Teacher's Edition
- Transparencies
- Assessment Masters
- Professional Development Guide
- ePresentation CD-ROM
- Teaching Tutor CD-ROM
- Online eSuite

The **Teacher's Edition** (spiral binding, hardback cover) contains the lessons for each unit. These lessons provide an instructional framework indicating what you should say and do in the program and how students

should respond. All pages in the student Content Reader appear in the Teacher's Edition, along with small reproductions of the transparencies/Workbook pages.

Twenty **transparencies** are used in the program. When you're asked to show a transparency to the class, the symbol 🖴 will appear in the Teacher's Edition.

The **Assessment Masters** provide blackline masters of the unit assessments and fluency passages as well as the Strategy Bookmarks (also found, in color and perforated, at the back of the Workbook). The Assessment Masters book also contains the Answer Key for the unit assessments and for the Workbook standardized tests. When you're directed to an Assessment Masters page, the symbol 📰 will appear in the Teacher's Edition.

This **Professional Development Guide** overviews the program, the instructional sequence used, the research base, and various teaching techniques. It includes sample lessons (Appendix A), the Placement Test (Appendix B), and information for training professional staff (Appendix C).

The **ePresentation CD-ROM** contains electronic transparencies, select electronic Workbook pages, and select electronic Assessment Masters pages for classroom display; these electronic slides correspond to each unit lesson. As you teach each lesson, using the Teacher's Edition as your guide, you have two choices when the script directs you to show a transparency, Workbook page, or Assessment Masters page: You may use the transparency set provided and discussed above, or you may use the ePresentation. A short instructional guide can be found on the ePresentation upon loading the CD-ROM. When you're instructed to show a transparency, Workbook page, or Assessment Masters page that is also available electronically on the ePresentation, the symbol 🔘 will appear in the Teacher's Edition.

The **Teaching Tutor CD-ROM** outlines skills and strategies (from the three tracks—comprehension, vocabulary, and fluency) taught at the beginning, middle, and end of the program. It includes informative slides as well as video demonstrations of a teacher and students using *Read to Achieve.* A downloadable training slide presentation is also on the Tutor.

The online **eSuite** allows you to plan your next lesson using an interactive calendar and electronic views of all materials in the program. Correlations to state standards are available, as are links to the ePresentation, the Teaching Tutor, and an electronic version of the Professional Development Guide.

Student Materials

Student materials consist of the following:

- Content Reader
- Workbook

The **Content Reader** is a nonconsumable textbook that contains 70 percent science lessons (Units 1 and 2, 5–8, 11–14, 17–20) and 30 percent social studies lessons (Units 3 and 4, 9 and 10, 15 and 16). Units 21–25 use classroom science (Units 21 and 22) and social studies (Units 23 and 24) textbooks; Unit 25 instructs teachers to choose either the science or social studies classroom text.

The **Workbook** is consumable and contains activities for each lesson. Activities progress from those requiring strong teacher support to those demonstrating student independence.

Read to Achieve Materials at a Glance									
Materials	**Teacher's Edition**	**Transparencies**	**Assessment Masters**	**Professional Development Guide**	**ePresentation CD-ROM**	**Teaching Tutor CD-ROM**	**eSuite**	**Content Reader**	**Workbook**
Teacher	X	X	X	X	X	X	X		
Student								X	X

Instructional Sequence

Instructional-Sequence Chart

The following chart illustrates how instruction is sequenced in **Read to Achieve** and how this sequence is labeled using teacher-support bars (Teacher's Edition) and Scope and Sequence symbols (Teacher's Edition and pages 16–21 of this guide). Teacher-support bars are found at the beginning of each activity in the Teacher's Edition; the appropriate level of teacher support is highlighted in red. The program provides strong teacher support when a skill or strategy is first taught. Over time, collaborative learning allows the level of support to fade until the student performs the skill or strategy on his or her own.

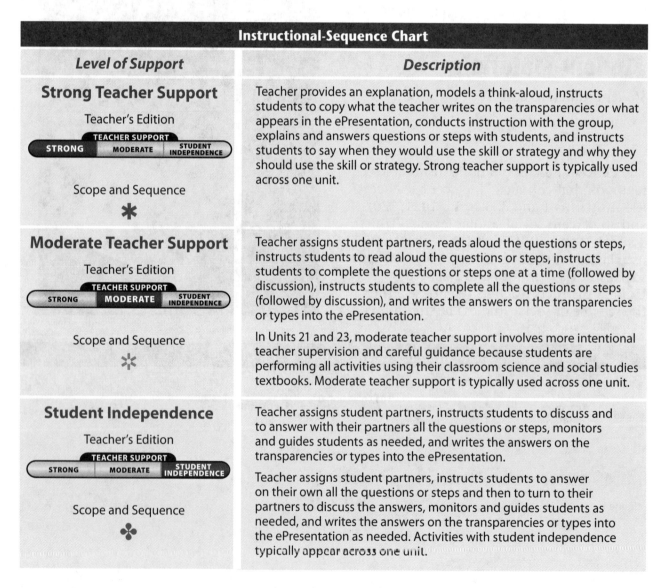

Instructional-Sequence Chart	
Level of Support	**Description**
Strong Teacher Support Teacher's Edition TEACHER SUPPORT STRONG / MODERATE / STUDENT INDEPENDENCE Scope and Sequence ✱	Teacher provides an explanation, models a think-aloud, instructs students to copy what the teacher writes on the transparencies or what appears in the ePresentation, conducts instruction with the group, explains and answers questions or steps with students, and instructs students to say when they would use the skill or strategy and why they should use the skill or strategy. Strong teacher support is typically used across one unit.
Moderate Teacher Support Teacher's Edition TEACHER SUPPORT STRONG / MODERATE / STUDENT INDEPENDENCE Scope and Sequence ✲	Teacher assigns student partners, reads aloud the questions or steps, instructs students to read aloud the questions or steps, instructs students to complete the questions or steps one at a time (followed by discussion), instructs students to complete all the questions or steps (followed by discussion), and writes the answers on the transparencies or types into the ePresentation. In Units 21 and 23, moderate teacher support involves more intentional teacher supervision and careful guidance because students are performing all activities using their classroom science and social studies textbooks. Moderate teacher support is typically used across one unit.
Student Independence Teacher's Edition TEACHER SUPPORT STRONG / MODERATE / STUDENT INDEPENDENCE Scope and Sequence ♣	Teacher assigns student partners, instructs students to discuss and to answer with their partners all the questions or steps, monitors and guides students as needed, and writes the answers on the transparencies or types into the ePresentation. Teacher assigns student partners, instructs students to answer on their own all the questions or steps and then to turn to their partners to discuss the answers, monitors and guides students as needed, and writes the answers on the transparencies or types into the ePresentation as needed. Activities with student independence typically appear across one unit.

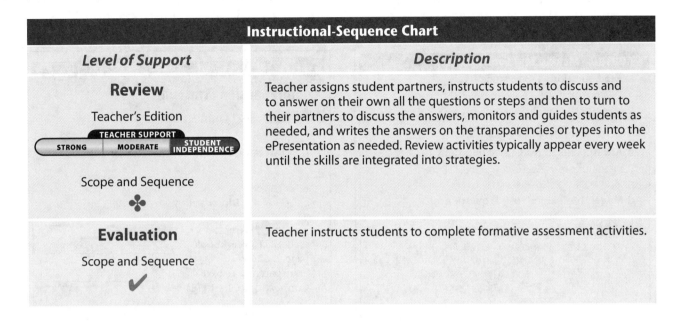

Instructional-Sequence Chart

Level of Support	Description
Review Teacher's Edition TEACHER SUPPORT STRONG — MODERATE — STUDENT INDEPENDENCE Scope and Sequence ♣	Teacher assigns student partners, instructs students to discuss and to answer on their own all the questions or steps and then to turn to their partners to discuss the answers, monitors and guides students as needed, and writes the answers on the transparencies or types into the ePresentation as needed. Review activities typically appear every week until the skills are integrated into strategies.
Evaluation Scope and Sequence ✔	Teacher instructs students to complete formative assessment activities.

Program Examples

The following lesson examples illustrate how teacher support is faded over time for all activities—in this case, for text-connections activities.

Unit 1, Lesson 1, Text Connections has strong teacher support and explicit instruction.

PART **A** ⏱ 20 minutes | STRONG | MODERATE | STUDENT INDEPENDENCE

Comprehension Strategies

Activity ▶ **Text Connections**

1. Before you begin reading a chapter or a section in your science or your social studies textbook, think about the topic of the chapter or the section. The topic is what the lesson is about. The topic is usually the title. Why is it important for you to know the topic of a chapter? **Accept** reasonable responses.

2. Besides thinking about the topic of a chapter or a section in your textbook, think about your purpose for reading the text. You should ask yourself why you're reading. You might say you're reading because the text is a class assignment, but why should you really be reading these science and social studies textbooks? **Accept** reasonable responses.

3. Finally, think about what you may already know about the topic. Doing this gets you interested in the text and helps you connect with it. Making these connections helps you relate to the text and makes reading it more enjoyable. Why does thinking about what you may already know about the text help you? **Accept** reasonable responses.

Strong Teacher Support

Teacher support is strong at the beginning of the program (**Unit 1, Lessons 1–5**), when students have not learned to make text connections.

4. 📖 **Direct** students to **Content Reader** page i.

5. The table of contents is essentially an outline of a book. It shows how the book is organized. It lists the units and lessons and their titles as well as the page numbers where the lessons are found. Find Unit 1, Lesson 1, and its page number in the table of contents. On what page will you find Unit 1, Lesson 1? 6. **Direct** students to page 6.

6. 🗑 💿 **Show** Transparency 1: Text-Connections Chart (T1).

Transparency 1

7. Today you'll learn to make text connections to help you understand what you read. In the next lesson, you'll use the Text-Connections Chart in your **Workbook** to help you make connections with what you'll read in your **Content Reader**.

ROUTINE · Making Text Connections

a. **Read** questions 1–3 to students.
- 1: What's the topic of the lesson?
- 2: What's your purpose for reading?
- 3: What do you know about the topic?

b. **Ask** students to read aloud questions 1–3.

c. I'll use the Text-Connections Chart to make connections with what I'll be reading.

d. **Model** think-aloud for T1: question 1.

Think-Aloud Question 1: First, I need to ask myself what the topic of the lesson is. The title of this lesson is "Studying Science." The title is usually the topic, so I'll write *Studying Science* after the first question, "What's the topic of the lesson?" ❖

e. Besides identifying the topic of the lesson, you should establish a purpose for reading it. When you read science and social studies lessons, your purpose for reading is to learn more about the topic.

f. **Model** think-aloud for T1: question 2.

Think-Aloud Question 2: Second, I need to ask myself, "What's my purpose for reading this lesson?" The topic of this lesson is studying science. My purpose for reading this lesson is to learn more about the topic, so my purpose for reading is to learn more about studying science. I'll write *to learn more about studying science* after the second question, "What's your purpose for reading?" ❖

g. After you identify the topic and a purpose for reading, think about what you may already know about the topic.

h. **Model** think-aloud for T1: question 3.

Think-Aloud Question 3: Third, I need to ask myself what I know about the topic. The topic of this lesson is studying science. I know some things about studying science. I know scientists study science, do experiments, and sometimes work in laboratories, so I'll write *Scientists study science, do experiments, and sometimes work in laboratories* after the third question, "What do you know about the topic?" ❖

8. When could you use the Text-Connections Chart? **Accept** reasonable responses.

9. Why should you use the Text-Connections Chart? **Accept** reasonable responses.

Teacher's Edition: Unit 1, Lesson 1

Unit 1, Lesson 2, Text Connections has strong teacher support and continued explicit instruction.

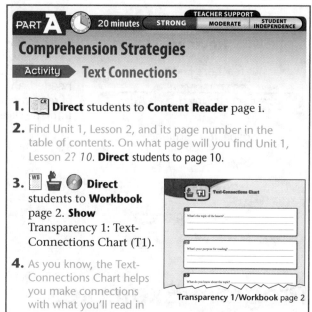

PART A ⏱ 20 minutes | STRONG | MODERATE | STUDENT INDEPENDENCE | TEACHER SUPPORT

Comprehension Strategies

Activity ▶ Text Connections

1. 📖 **Direct** students to **Content Reader** page i.

2. Find Unit 1, Lesson 2, and its page number in the table of contents. On what page will you find Unit 1, Lesson 2? *10.* **Direct** students to page 10.

3. **Direct** students to **Workbook** page 2. **Show** Transparency 1: Text-Connections Chart (T1).

4. As you know, the Text-Connections Chart helps you make connections with what you'll read in your **Content Reader**.

Transparency 1/Workbook page 2

ROUTINE · Making Text Connections

a. **Read** questions 1–3 to students.
- Question 1: What's the topic of the lesson?
- Question 2: What's your purpose for reading?
- Question 3: What do you know about the topic?

b. **Ask** students to read aloud questions 1–3.

c. **Have** students copy everything you write as you model think-aloud for T1: question 1.

Think-Aloud Question 1: First, I need to ask myself what the topic of the lesson is. The title of this lesson is "The Scientific Process." The title is usually the topic, so I'll write *The Scientific Process* after the first question, "What's the topic of the lesson?" ❖

d. Besides identifying the topic of the lesson, you should establish a purpose for reading it. Your purpose for reading is to learn more about the topic.

e. **Model** think-aloud for T1: question 2.

Think-Aloud Question 2: Second, I need to ask myself, "What's my purpose for reading this lesson?" The topic of this lesson is the scientific process. My purpose for reading this lesson is to learn more about my topic, so my purpose for reading is to learn more about the scientific process. I'll write *to learn more about the scientific process* after the second question, "What's your purpose for reading?" ❖

f. Besides identifying the topic and a purpose for reading, think about what you may already know about the topic.

g. **Model** think-aloud for T1: question 3.

> **Think-Aloud** Question 3: Third, I need to ask myself what I know about the topic. The topic of this lesson is the scientific process. I know some things about the scientific process. I know scientists first make a guess or hypothesis about what will happen when they do an experiment. I also know scientists use their findings to conduct future experiments, so I'll write what I know about the scientific process after the third question, "What do you know about the topic?" ❖

5. What do you know about the scientific process? **Accept** reasonable responses.

6. When could you use the Text-Connections Chart? **Accept** reasonable responses.

7. Why should you use the Text-Connections Chart? **Accept** reasonable responses.

Teacher's Edition: Unit 1, Lesson 2

Unit 1, Lesson 3, Text Connections has strong teacher support and fading explicit instruction.

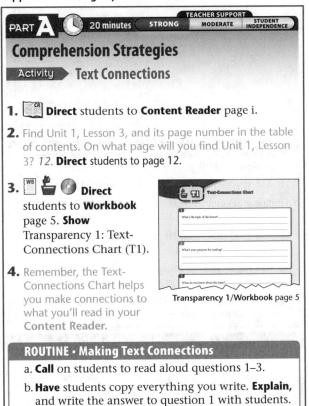

PART **A** 🕐 20 minutes | TEACHER SUPPORT **STRONG** MODERATE | STUDENT INDEPENDENCE

Comprehension Strategies

Activity Text Connections

1. 📖 **Direct** students to **Content Reader** page i.

2. Find Unit 1, Lesson 3, and its page number in the table of contents. On what page will you find Unit 1, Lesson 3? *12.* **Direct** students to page 12.

3. 📓🪴💿 **Direct** students to **Workbook** page 5. **Show** Transparency 1: Text-Connections Chart (T1).

4. Remember, the Text-Connections Chart helps you make connections to what you'll read in your **Content Reader**.

Transparency 1/Workbook page 5

ROUTINE • Making Text Connections

a. **Call** on students to read aloud questions 1–3.

b. **Have** students copy everything you write. **Explain,** and write the answer to question 1 with students. *Technology*

c. **Explain,** and write the answer to question 2 with students. *to learn more about technology*

d. **Explain,** and write the answer to question 3 with students. **Accept** reasonable responses.

Teacher's Edition: Unit 1, Lesson 3

Unit 1, Lesson 4, Text Connections has strong teacher support and fading explicit instruction.

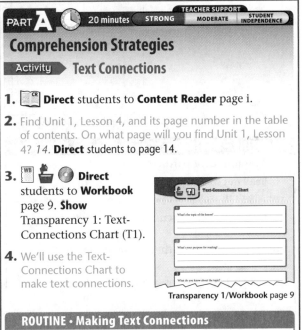

PART **A** 🕐 20 minutes | TEACHER SUPPORT **STRONG** MODERATE | STUDENT INDEPENDENCE

Comprehension Strategies

Activity Text Connections

1. 📖 **Direct** students to **Content Reader** page i.

2. Find Unit 1, Lesson 4, and its page number in the table of contents. On what page will you find Unit 1, Lesson 4? *14.* **Direct** students to page 14.

3. 📓🪴💿 **Direct** students to **Workbook** page 9. **Show** Transparency 1: Text-Connections Chart (T1).

4. We'll use the Text-Connections Chart to make text connections.

Transparency 1/Workbook page 9

ROUTINE • Making Text Connections

a. **Ask** students to read aloud question 1.

b. **Have** students copy everything you write. **Write** the answer to question 1 with students. *Safety in the Laboratory*

c. **Repeat** steps a and b for question 2. *to learn more about safety in the laboratory*

d. **Repeat** steps a and b for question 3. **Accept** reasonable responses.

Teacher's Edition: Unit 1, Lesson 4

Moderate Teacher Support

As the program continues (**Unit 2**), text-connections activities begin to gradually fade.

Unit 2, Lesson 1, Text Connections has moderate teacher support and some student application.

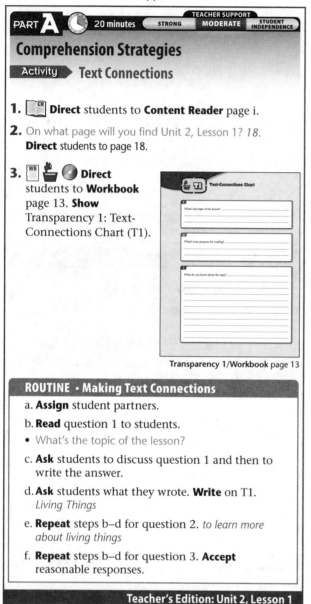

Transparency 1/Workbook page 13

ROUTINE • Making Text Connections

a. **Assign** student partners.

b. **Read** question 1 to students.

• What's the topic of the lesson?

c. **Ask** students to discuss question 1 and then to write the answer.

d. **Ask** students what they wrote. **Write** on T1. *Living Things*

e. **Repeat** steps b–d for question 2. *to learn more about living things*

f. **Repeat** steps b–d for question 3. **Accept** reasonable responses.

Teacher's Edition: Unit 2, Lesson 1

Unit 2, Lesson 2, Text Connections has moderate teacher support and some continued student application.

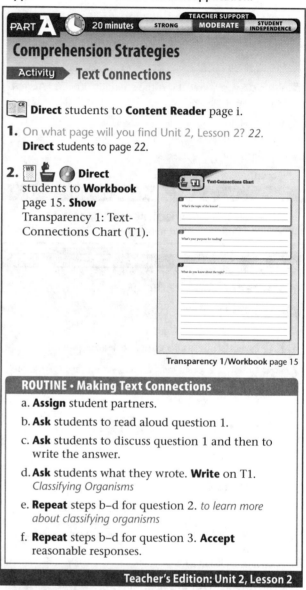

Transparency 1/Workbook page 15

ROUTINE • Making Text Connections

a. **Assign** student partners.

b. **Ask** students to read aloud question 1.

c. **Ask** students to discuss question 1 and then to write the answer.

d. **Ask** students what they wrote. **Write** on T1. *Classifying Organisms*

e. **Repeat** steps b–d for question 2. *to learn more about classifying organisms*

f. **Repeat** steps b–d for question 3. **Accept** reasonable responses.

Teacher's Edition: Unit 2, Lesson 2

All levels of Bloom's Taxonomy are woven into activities.

Unit 2, Lesson 3, Text Connections has moderate teacher support and some continued student application.

Unit 2, Lesson 4, Text Connections has moderate teacher support and some continued student application.

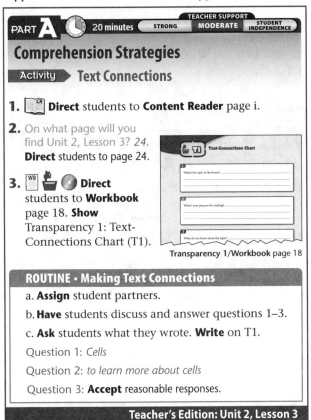

Transparency 1/Workbook page 18

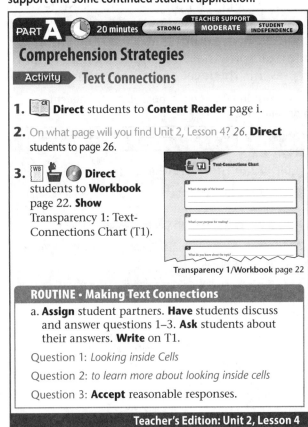

Transparency 1/Workbook page 22

Student Independence

As the program continues (**Units 3–5**), text-connections activities are again gradually faded to the point where students make text connections on their own and then discuss their findings with their partners. In the examples that follow, the level of support in Lesson 1 of each unit represents the level of support in Lessons 2–4 of each unit.

Unit 3, Lesson 1, Text Connections allows for student independence.

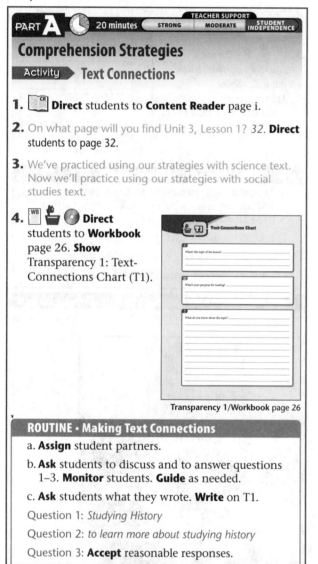

Transparency 1/Workbook page 26

ROUTINE · Making Text Connections

a. **Assign** student partners.

b. **Ask** students to discuss and to answer questions 1–3. **Monitor** students. **Guide** as needed.

c. **Ask** students what they wrote. **Write** on T1.

Question 1: *Studying History*

Question 2: *to learn more about studying history*

Question 3: **Accept** reasonable responses.

Teacher's Edition: Unit 3, Lesson 1

Unit 4, Lesson 1, Text Connections allows for further student independence.

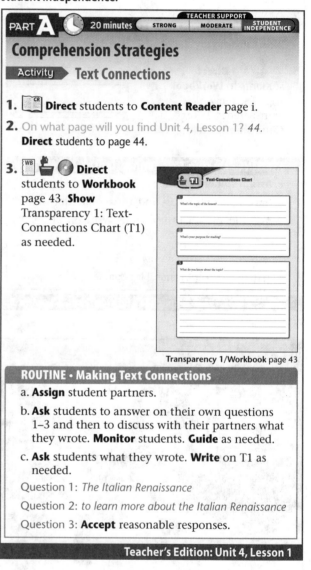

Transparency 1/Workbook page 43

ROUTINE · Making Text Connections

a. **Assign** student partners.

b. **Ask** students to answer on their own questions 1–3 and then to discuss with their partners what they wrote. **Monitor** students. **Guide** as needed.

c. **Ask** students what they wrote. **Write** on T1 as needed.

Question 1: *The Italian Renaissance*

Question 2: *to learn more about the Italian Renaissance*

Question 3: **Accept** reasonable responses.

Teacher's Edition: Unit 4, Lesson 1

Unit 5, Lesson 1, Text Connections allows for further student independence.

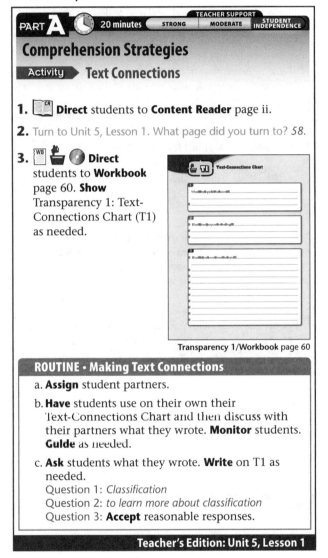

Comprehension Strategies

Activity ▶ **Text Connections**

1. 📖 **Direct** students to **Content Reader** page ii.

2. Turn to Unit 5, Lesson 1. What page did you turn to? *58*.

3. 🖥 🌐 **Direct** students to **Workbook** page 60. **Show** Transparency 1: Text-Connections Chart (T1) as needed.

Text-Connections Chart

Transparency 1/Workbook page 60

ROUTINE · Making Text Connections

a. **Assign** student partners.

b. **Have** students use on their own their Text-Connections Chart and then discuss with their partners what they wrote. **Monitor** students. **Guide** as needed.

c. **Ask** students what they wrote. **Write** on T1 as needed.
Question 1: *Classification*
Question 2: *to learn more about classification*
Question 3: **Accept** reasonable responses.

Teacher's Edition: Unit 5, Lesson 1

The text-connections activity is reviewed in subsequent units until—in **Unit 8, Lesson 1,** below—the skill is folded into a more complex strategy, the SQ3R strategy.

Unit 8, Lesson 1, integrates text connections with the SQ3R strategy.

Comprehension Strategies

Activity ▶ **SQ3R Strategy: Survey**

1. In your science and social studies classes, you usually have to read and study chapters or sections from your science and social studies textbooks. How do you usually read and study for science and social studies classes now? **Accept** reasonable responses.

2. Chapters or sections in your science and social studies textbooks, and lessons in your **Content Reader,** have special features to help you gather important information. You'll find these special features when you begin reading a chapter, section, or lesson; while you're reading the main part of the chapter, section, or lesson; and at the end of the chapter, section, or lesson.

3. 📖 **Direct** students to **Content Reader** page ii.

4. Turn to Unit 8, Lesson 1. What page did you turn to? *94*.

5. Today you'll learn a strategy to help you gather important information from lessons in your **Content Reader.** This strategy will also be helpful when you read your science and social studies textbooks. This strategy is called SQ3R.

6. Show Transparency 12: SQ3R-Strategy Checklist (T12).

7. Each letter of the SQ3R strategy stands for something. **Point** to each part of the checklist as you read. The *S* stands for "Survey," the *Q* stands for "Question," the first *R* stands for "Read," the second *R* stands for "Reflect," and the third *R* stands for "Review." First, you'll learn to survey a lesson in your **Content Reader.**

Transparency 12

ROUTINE · Using the SQ3R Strategy: Survey

a. **Read** "Survey" steps 1–4 to students.
- Step 1: Make text connections.
- Step 2: Read the beginning of the lesson.
- Step 3: Look at the main part of the lesson.
- Step 4: Read the end of the lesson.

b. **Ask** students to read aloud "Survey" steps 1–4.

c. You've completed Step 1 before. For the SQ3R strategy, you'll make text connections as part of a larger strategy.

d. **Ask** students to read Step 1 questions 1–3.

e. **Assign** student partners.

f. **Have** students make text connections on their own and then discuss with their partners what connections they made. **Monitor** students. **Guide** as needed.

g. **Ask** students what text connections they made.

Question 1: *Matter: Mass, Weight, and Volume*

Question 2: *to learn more about the mass, weight, and volume of matter*

Question 3: **Accept** reasonable responses.

h. **Make** a check mark in the "Yes" box next to Step 1.

i. I'll use the SQ3R strategy to complete the remaining three "Survey" steps. Follow along in your **Content Reader.**

j. **Model** think-aloud for T12: "Survey" Step 2.

Think-Aloud "Survey" Step 2: The lesson is about the mass, weight, and volume of matter, and my purpose for reading is to learn more about the mass, weight, and volume of matter. For Step 2, I need to read, or survey, special features at the beginning of the lesson other than the title or the topic. I'll survey the sidebars, which are the boxes with text that are next to the main lesson text. The sidebar on the first page of the lesson shows some important information. It shows what I'll learn, why it's important, and what the key terms are. **Point** at the sidebar on **Content Reader** page 94, and read the text to students. This sidebar special feature gives me a good idea about what I should be thinking about and taking notes on when I read my lesson. It looks like I'll be learning a lot about matter. Now I need to use my SQ3R-Strategy Checklist. Because I surveyed the beginning of the lesson, I'll go to the column labeled "Yes" and make a check mark in the box next to Step 2 of "Survey." **Make** a check mark in the "Yes" box next to Step 2. ❖

k. **Model** think-aloud for T12: "Survey" Step 3.

Think-Aloud "Survey" Step 3: For Step 3, I need to read, or survey, the special features in the main part of the lesson. I'll survey and think about the title and subheads, the bold and highlighted words, and the pictures, graphs, charts, and captions. **Point** at these types of text features, and read or describe them to students. These special features give me a good idea about how my lesson is organized. They show more specific information about what I'll be learning. Now I need to use my SQ3R-Strategy Checklist. Because I surveyed the main part of the lesson, I'll go to the column labeled "Yes" and make a check mark in the box next to Step 3 of "Survey." **Make** a check mark in the "Yes" box next to Step 3. ❖

l. **Model** think-aloud for T12: "Survey" Step 4.

Think-Aloud "Survey" Step 4: For Step 4, I need to survey the special features found at the end of the lesson. I'll survey and think about the lesson assessment, which is another sidebar. This assessment includes review, critical thinking, and writing-in-science questions. **Point** at the sidebar on **Content Reader** page 97, and read the text to students. These special features give me a good idea about what I'm expected to learn from this lesson. If I can answer these questions after reading the lesson, I have a good understanding of what the lesson is about. Now I need to use my SQ3R-Strategy Checklist. Because I surveyed the end of the lesson, I'll go to the column labeled "Yes" and make a check mark in the box next to Step 4 of "Survey." **Make** a check mark in the "Yes" box next to Step 4. ❖

8. When could you survey your lesson? **Accept** reasonable responses.

9. Why should you survey your lesson? **Accept** reasonable responses.

Teacher's Edition: Unit 8, Lesson 1

In **Unit 22, Lesson 1,** students use their classroom science textbook and the Strategy Bookmark to work through text connections.

Unit 22, Lesson 1, allows students to apply text connections to their classroom textbook.

PART A ⏱ **25 minutes** | STRONG | MODERATE | STUDENT INDEPENDENCE

Comprehension Strategies

Activity ▶ Strategy Bookmark: Comprehension Strategies

1. 📑 **Direct** students to retrieve their green Strategy Bookmark from their science textbook.

Transparency 13

ROUTINE • Using the Strategy Bookmark: SQ3R Strategy

a. **Assign** student partners.

b. 🧺 💿 **Show** Transparency 13: Note-Taking Form (T13). **Provide** notebook paper to students. **Have** students set up the paper for SQ3R notes.

c. **Direct** students to the beginning of the textbook section. **Assign** the total number of pages to be read.

d. **Have** students refer to the Strategy Bookmark as they complete on their own all SQ3R steps, look for text structure, and then discuss with their partners. **Have** students continue the process until they finish the section. **Monitor** students. **Guide** as needed.

e. **Ask** students to describe how they completed the SQ3R strategy. **Accept** reasonable responses.

f. **Ask** students what they did. **Write** on T13 as needed. (When you have completed this activity, **retain** T13 with any written notes for the next activity.)

Teacher's Edition: Unit 22, Lesson 1

Text-connections activities are woven into "Beyond the Book" extension activities (for example, "**Beyond the Book**" **Units 1 and 2**). These activities involve classroom science and social studies textbooks, as well as other informational text.

"Beyond the Book" Units 1 and 2 allows students to apply text connections to informational text.

Informational Text

Activity ▶ Topic Connections

Topic

1. **Describe** to students how the science topics they've read about in Units 1 and 2 can be found in outside sources such as newspapers. **Explain** how students can use the reading skills and strategies they learned in Units 1 and 2 to better read and comprehend newspaper articles about science.

2. 📖 **Direct** students to **Content Reader** page 30. Using what students have learned about making text connections, **ask** three questions about the newspaper article. Questions might focus on the topic of the article, the purpose for reading the article, and what students already know about lab explosions.

Activity ▶ Media Connections

Medium

1. 📖 **Direct** students to **Content Reader** page 30. **Have** students read the newspaper article.

2. **Assign** student partners.

3. **Explain** that reporters create newspaper articles by performing research and interviewing others. Students will now do an interview activity. One partner will be a reporter asking questions, and one will be a witness to the lab explosion. Reporters may want to ask questions such as, "What happened?" or, "How could this accident have been prevented?" Witnesses will want to make sure they have a good understanding of the events so they can give accurate answers. **Allow** six minutes. **Have** partners then switch roles.

4. **Have** students use the decoding-multipart-words strategy on five multipart words they find in the newspaper article. **Tell** students to complete the activity on notebook paper.

Teacher's Edition: Beyond the Book, Units 1 and 2

Scope and Sequence

SKILLS	Unit 1					Unit 2					Unit 3					Unit 4				
Lessons	1	2	3	4	5	1	2	3	4	5	1	2	3	4	5	1	2	3	4	5
CONTENT-AREA TEXT	Science										Social Studies									
COMPREHENSION STRATEGIES																				
TEXT FEATURES	■	■	■	■	■	■	■	■	■	■	■	■	■	■	■	■	■	■	■	■
TEXT CONNECTIONS																				
Identify Topic	*	*	*	*		✳	✳	✳	✳	✔	✤	✤	✤	✤	✔	✤	✤	✤	✤	✔
Establish Purpose for Reading	*	*	*	*		✳	✳	✳	✳	✔	✤	✤	✤	✤	✔	✤	✤	✤	✤	✔
Activate Prior Knowledge	*	*	*	*		✳	✳	✳	✳	✔	✤	✤	✤	✤	✔	✤	✤	✤	✤	✔
TEXT STRUCTURE																				
Description-or-List						*	*	*	*		*	*	*	*		✳	✳	✳	✳	✔
Order-or-Sequence						*	*	*	*		*	*	*	*		✳	✳	✳	✳	✔
Cause-and-Effect						*	*	*	*		*	*	*	*		✳	✳	✳	✳	✔
Compare-and-Contrast						*	*	*	*		*	*	*	*		✳	✳	✳	✳	✔
COMPREHENSION MONITORING *(begins at Unit 6)*																				
Reread and Adjust Reading Rate																				
SQ3R STRATEGY *(begins at Unit 8)*																				
Survey																				
Question																				
Read																				
Reflect																				
Review																				
QHL STRATEGY *(begins at Unit 15)*																				
What Questions do I have?																				
How will I find the answers?																				
What did I Learn after finding the answers?																				
NOTE TAKING *(begins at Unit 17)*																				
Lecture Notes																				
STRATEGY BOOKMARK *(begins at Unit 18)*																				
VOCABULARY STRATEGIES																				
Decoding Multipart Words	*	*	*	*		✳	✳	✳	✳	✔	✤	✤	✤	✤	✔	✤	✤	✤	✤	✔
WORD-LEARNING STRATEGIES																				
Context Clues						*	*	*	*		✳	✳	✳	✳	✔	✤	✤	✤	✤	✔
Glossary Use																				
Dictionary Use																				
Online-Dictionary Use																				
STRATEGY BOOKMARK *(begins at Unit 18)*																				
HIGHER-ORDER THINKING																				
Bloom's Taxonomy/ Standardized-Test Practice		✔		✔			✔		✔			✔		✔			✔		✔	
Graphic Organizer	■	■	■	■	■	■	■	■	■	■	■	■	■	■	■	■	■	■	■	■
Metacognition	■	■	■	■	■	■	■	■	■	■	■	■	■	■	■	■	■	■	■	■
FLUENCY STRATEGIES																				
Oral Reading	✔		■	✔	✔			■	✔	✔	✔		■	✔	✔				■	✔
Silent Reading		■	■				■	■				■	■					■		
DIFFERENTIATED INSTRUCTION/RESPONSE TO INTERVENTION																				
Strategies and Tips										■					■					■

✱ = Strong Teacher Support   ✳ = Moderate Teacher Support   ✤ = Student Independence   ■ = Practiced   ✔ = Knowledge/Evaluative Check

SKILLS	Unit 5					Unit 6					Unit 7					Unit 8				
Lessons	1	2	3	4	5	1	2	3	4	5	1	2	3	4	5	1	2	3	4	5
CONTENT-AREA TEXT	Science																			
COMPREHENSION STRATEGIES																				
TEXT FEATURES	■	■	■	■	■	■	■	■	■	■	■	■	■	■	■	■	■	■	■	■
TEXT CONNECTIONS																				
Identify Topic	❖			✔	❖				✔	❖						❖	❖	❖	❖	✔
Establish Purpose for Reading	❖			✔	❖				✔	❖						❖	❖	❖	❖	✔
Activate Prior Knowledge	❖			✔	❖				✔	❖						❖	❖	❖	❖	✔
TEXT STRUCTURE																				
Description-or-List	✸	✸	✸	✸	✔	❖	❖	❖	❖	✔	❖	❖	❖	❖	✔				❖	✔
Order-or-Sequence	✸	✸	✸	✸	✔	❖	❖	❖	❖	✔	❖	❖	❖	❖	✔				❖	✔
Cause-and-Effect	✸	✸	✸	✸	✔	❖	❖	❖	❖	✔	❖	❖	❖	❖	✔				❖	✔
Compare-and-Contrast	✸	✸	✸	✸	✔	❖	❖	❖	❖	✔	❖	❖	❖	❖	✔				❖	✔
COMPREHENSION MONITORING																				
Reread and Adjust Reading Rate						✹	✹	✹	✹		✸	✸	✸	✸	✔	❖	❖	❖	❖	✔
SQ3R STRATEGY																				
Survey																✹	✹	✹	✹	
Question																				
Read																				
Reflect																				
Review																				
QHL STRATEGY *(begins at Unit 15)*																				
What **Q**uestions do I have?																				
How will I find the answers?																				
What did I **L**earn after finding the answers?																				
NOTE TAKING *(begins at Unit 17)*																				
Lecture Notes																				
STRATEGY BOOKMARK *(begins at Unit 18)*																				
VOCABULARY STRATEGIES																				
Decoding Multipart Words	❖	❖	❖	❖	✔		❖			✔		❖			✔		❖			
WORD-LEARNING STRATEGIES																				
Context Clues	❖	❖	❖	❖	✔		❖			✔		❖			✔		❖			
Glossary Use							✹	✹	✹	✹	✸	✸	✸	✸	✔	❖	❖	❖	❖	✔
Dictionary Use											✹	✹	✹	✹		✸	✸	✸	✸	✔
Online-Dictionary Use																✹	✹	✹	✹	
STRATEGY BOOKMARK *(begins at Unit 18)*																				
HIGHER-ORDER THINKING																				
Bloom's Taxonomy/ Standardized-Test Practice		✔		✔			✔		✔			✔		✔			✔		✔	✔
Graphic Organizer	■	■	■	■	■	■	■	■	■	■	■	■	■	■	■	■	■	■	■	■
Metacognition	■	■	■	■	■	■	■	■	■	■	■	■	■	■	■	■	■	■	■	■
FLUENCY STRATEGIES																				
Oral Reading	✔		■	✔	✔		■		✔	✔			■	✔	✔			■		✔
Silent Reading			■	■			■	■				■	■				■	■		
DIFFERENTIATED INSTRUCTION/RESPONSE TO INTERVENTION																				
Strategies and Tips					■					■					■					■

✹ = Strong Teacher Support ✸ = Moderate Teacher Support ❖ = Student Independence ■ = Practiced ✔ = Knowledge/Evaluative Check

SKILLS / CONTENT-AREA TEXT	Unit 9 — Social Studies					Unit 10 — Social Studies					Unit 11 — Science					Unit 12 — Science				
Lessons	1	2	3	4	5	1	2	3	4	5	1	2	3	4	5	1	2	3	4	5
COMPREHENSION STRATEGIES																				
TEXT FEATURES	■	■	■	■	■	■	■	■	■	■	■	■	■	■	■	■	■	■	■	■
TEXT CONNECTIONS																				
Identify Topic	✿	✿	✿	✿	✔	✿	✿	✿	✿	✔	✿	✿	✿	✿	✔	✿	✿	✿	✿	✔
Establish Purpose for Reading	✿	✿	✿	✿	✔	✿	✿	✿	✿	✔	✿	✿	✿	✿	✔	✿	✿	✿	✿	✔
Activate Prior Knowledge	✿	✿	✿	✿	✔	✿	✿	✿	✿	✔	✿	✿	✿	✿	✔	✿	✿	✿	✿	✔
TEXT STRUCTURE																				
Description-or-List				✿	✔				✿					✿	✔				✿	
Order-or-Sequence				✿	✔				✿					✿	✔				✿	
Cause-and-Effect				✿	✔				✿					✿	✔				✿	
Compare-and-Contrast				✿	✔				✿					✿	✔				✿	
COMPREHENSION MONITORING																				
Reread and Adjust Reading Rate	✿	✿	✿	✿	✔	✿	✿	✿	✿	✔	✿	✿	✿	✿	✔	✿	✿	✿	✿	✔
SQ3R STRATEGY																				
Survey	✳	✳	✳	✳	✔	✿	✿	✿	✿	✔	✿	✿	✿	✿	✔	✿	✿	✿	✿	✔
Question	✳	✳	✳	✳		✳	✳	✳	✳		✿	✿	✿	✿	✔	✿	✿	✿	✿	✔
Read	✳	✳	✳	✳		✳	✳	✳	✳	✔	✿	✿	✿	✿	✔	✿	✿	✿	✿	✔
Reflect							✳	✳	✳	✳	✳	✳	✳	✳	✔	✿	✿	✿	✿	✔
Review											✳	✳	✳	✳		✳	✳	✳	✳	✔
QHL STRATEGY *(begins at Unit 15)*																				
What **Q**uestions do I have?																				
How will I find the answers?																				
What did I **L**earn after finding the answers?																				
NOTE TAKING *(begins at Unit 17)*																				
Lecture Notes																				
STRATEGY BOOKMARK *(begins at Unit 18)*																				
VOCABULARY STRATEGIES																				
Decoding Multipart Words		✿				✔		✿						✿		✔		✿		
WORD-LEARNING STRATEGIES																				
Context Clues	✿	✿	✿	✿	✔	✿	✿	✿	✿	✔	✿	✿	✿	✿	✔	✿	✿	✿	✿	✔
Glossary Use	✿	✿	✿	✿	✔				✔		✿			✔		✿				
Dictionary Use	✿	✿	✿	✿	✔					✔		✿		✔						✔
Online-Dictionary Use	✳	✳	✳	✳	✔	✿	✿	✿	✿	✔	✿	✿	✿	✿	✔			✿		✔
STRATEGY BOOKMARK *(begins at Unit 18)*																				
HIGHER-ORDER THINKING																				
Bloom's Taxonomy/ Standardized-Test Practice		✔		✔			✔		✔			✔		✔			✔		✔	
Graphic Organizer	■	■	■	■	■	■	■	■	■	■	■	■	■	■	■	■	■	■	■	■
Metacognition	■	■	■	■	■	■	■	■	■	■	■	■	■	■	■	■	■	■	■	■
FLUENCY STRATEGIES																				
Oral Reading	✔		■	✔	✔			■	✔	✔	✔		■	✔	✔			■		✔
Silent Reading		■	■					■	■				■	■				■	■	
DIFFERENTIATED INSTRUCTION/RESPONSE TO INTERVENTION																				
Strategies and Tips			■					■						■						■

✳ = Strong Teacher Support   ✿ = Moderate Teacher Support   ✢ = Student Independence   ■ = Practiced   ✔ = Knowledge/Evaluative Check

SKILLS / Lessons	U13·1	U13·2	U13·3	U13·4	U13·5	U14·1	U14·2	U14·3	U14·4	U14·5	U15·1	U15·2	U15·3	U15·4	U15·5	U16·1	U16·2	U16·3	U16·4	U16·5
CONTENT-AREA TEXT	Science										Social Studies									
COMPREHENSION STRATEGIES																				
TEXT FEATURES	■	■	■	■	■	■	■	■	■	■	■	■	■	■	■	■	■	■	■	■
TEXT CONNECTIONS																				
Identify Topic	✤	✤	✤	✤	✔	✤	✤	✤	✤	✔	✤	✤	✤	✤	✔	✤	✤	✤	✤	✔
Establish Purpose for Reading	✤	✤	✤	✤	✔	✤	✤	✤	✤	✔	✤	✤	✤	✤	✔	✤	✤	✤	✤	✔
Activate Prior Knowledge	✤	✤	✤	✤	✔	✤	✤	✤	✤	✔	✤	✤	✤	✤	✔	✤	✤	✤	✤	✔
TEXT STRUCTURE																				
Description-or-List			✤	✔					✤		✤	✤	✤	✤	✔	✤	✤	✤	✤	
Order-or-Sequence			✤	✔							✤	✤	✤	✤	✔	✤	✤	✤	✤	
Cause-and-Effect			✤	✔					✤		✤	✤	✤	✤	✔	✤	✤	✤	✤	
Compare-and-Contrast			✤	✔					✤		✤	✤	✤	✤	✤	✤	✤	✤		
COMPREHENSION MONITORING																				
Reread and Adjust Reading Rate	✤	✤	✤	✤	✔	✤	✤	✤	✤	✔	✤	✤	✤	✤	✔	✤	✤	✤	✤	✔
SQ3R STRATEGY																				
Survey	✤	✤	✤	✤	✔	✤	✤	✤	✤	✔	✤	✤	✤	✤	✔	✤	✤	✤	✤	✔
Question	✤	✤	✤	✤	✔	✤	✤	✤	✤	✔	✤	✤	✤	✤	✔	✤	✤	✤	✤	✔
Read	✤	✤	✤	✤	✔	✤	✤	✤	✤	✔	✤	✤	✤	✤	✔	✤	✤	✤	✤	✔
Reflect	✤	✤	✤	✤	✔	✤	✤	✤	✤	✔	✤	✤	✤	✤	✔	✤	✤	✤	✤	✔
Review	✤	✤	✤	✤	✔	✤	✤	✤	✤	✔	✤	✤	✤	✤	✔	✤	✤	✤	✤	✔
QHL STRATEGY																				
What Questions do I have?											✳	✳	✳	✳		✴	✴	✴	✴	✔
How will I find the answers?											✳	✳	✳	✳		✴	✴	✴	✴	✔
What did I Learn after finding the answers?											✳	✳	✳	✳		✴	✴	✴	✴	✔
NOTE TAKING *(begins at Unit 17)*																				
Lecture Notes																				
STRATEGY BOOKMARK *(begins at Unit 18)*																				
VOCABULARY STRATEGIES																				
Decoding Multipart Words		✤				✔		✤				✤				✔		✤		
WORD-LEARNING STRATEGIES																				
Context Clues	✤	✤	✤	✤	✔	✤	✤	✤	✤	✔	✤	✤	✤	✤	✔	✤	✤	✤	✤	✔
Glossary Use	✤			✔	✤						✤			✔	✤					
Dictionary Use		✤						✤		✔	✤							✤		✔
Online-Dictionary Use			✤					✤		✔		✤							✤	✔
STRATEGY BOOKMARK *(begins at Unit 18)*																				
HIGHER-ORDER THINKING																				
Bloom's Taxonomy / Standardized-Test Practice		✔		✔			✔		✔			✔		✔			✔		✔	
Graphic Organizer	■	■	■	■	■	■	■	■	■	■	■	■	■	■	■	■	■	■	■	■
Metacognition	■	■	■	■	■	■	■	■	■	■	■	■	■	■	■	■	■	■	■	■
FLUENCY STRATEGIES																				
Oral Reading	✔		■	✔	✔			■	✔	✔	✔		■	✔	✔				■	✔
Silent Reading		■	■					■	■			■	■					■	■	
DIFFERENTIATED INSTRUCTION/RESPONSE TO INTERVENTION																				
Strategies and Tips						■				■					■					■

✳ = Strong Teacher Support   ✴ = Moderate Teacher Support   ✤ = Student Independence   ■ = Practiced   ✔ = Knowledge/Evaluative Check

SKILLS	Unit 17					Unit 18					Unit 19					Unit 20				
Lessons	1	2	3	4	5	1	2	3	4	5	1	2	3	4	5	1	2	3	4	5
CONTENT-AREA TEXT	Science																			
COMPREHENSION STRATEGIES																				
TEXT FEATURES	■	■	■	■	■	■	■	■	■	■	■	■	■	■	■	■	■	■	■	■
TEXT CONNECTIONS																				
Identify Topic	✤	✤	✤	✤	✔	✤	✤	✤	✤	✔	✤	✤	✤	✤	✔	✤	✤	✤	✤	✔
Establish Purpose for Reading	✤	✤	✤	✤	✔	✤	✤	✤	✤	✔	✤	✤	✤	✤	✔	✤	✤	✤	✤	✔
Activate Prior Knowledge	✤	✤	✤	✤	✔	✤	✤	✤	✤	✔	✤	✤	✤	✤	✔	✤	✤	✤	✤	✔
TEXT STRUCTURE																				
Description-or-List	✤	✤	✤	✔		✤	✤	✤	✤		✤	✤	✤	✔		✤	✤	✤	✤	
Order-or-Sequence	✤	✤	✤	✔		✤	✤	✤	✤		✤	✤	✤	✔		✤	✤	✤	✤	
Cause-and-Effect	✤	✤	✤	✔		✤	✤	✤	✤		✤	✤	✤	✔		✤	✤	✤	✤	
Compare-and-Contrast	✤	✤	✤	✔		✤	✤	✤	✤		✤	✤	✤	✔		✤	✤	✤	✤	
COMPREHENSION MONITORING																				
Reread and Adjust Reading Rate	✤	✤	✤	✤	✔	✤	✤	✤	✤	✤	✤	✤	✤	✤	✔	✤	✤	✤	✤	✔
SQ3R STRATEGY																				
Survey	✤	✤	✤	✤	✔	✤	✤	✤	✤	✔	✤	✤	✤	✤	✔	✤	✤	✤	✤	✔
Question	✤	✤	✤	✤	✔	✤	✤	✤	✤	✔	✤	✤	✤	✤	✔	✤	✤	✤	✤	✔
Read	✤	✤	✤	✤	✔	✤	✤	✤	✤	✔	✤	✤	✤	✤	✔	✤	✤	✤	✤	✔
Reflect	✤	✤	✤	✤	✔	✤	✤	✤	✤	✔	✤	✤	✤	✤	✔	✤	✤	✤	✤	✔
Review	✤	✤	✤	✤	✔	✤	✤	✤	✤	✔	✤	✤	✤	✤	✔	✤	✤	✤	✤	✔
QHL STRATEGY																				
What Questions do I have?	✤	✤	✤	✤	✔	✤	✤	✤	✤	✤	✤	✤	✤	✤	✤	✤	✤	✤	✤	✔
How will I find the answers?	✤	✤	✤	✤	✔	✤	✤	✤	✤	✔	✤	✤	✤	✤	✤	✤	✤	✤	✤	✔
What did I Learn after finding the answers?	✤	✤	✤	✤		✤	✤	✤	✤	✔	✤	✤	✤	✤		✤	✤	✤	✤	✔
NOTE TAKING																				
Lecture Notes	✱	✱	✱	✱		✻	✻	✻	✻	✔	✤	✤	✤	✤	✔	✤	✤	✤	✤	✔
STRATEGY BOOKMARK						✻	✻	✻	✻	✔	✤	✤	✤	✤	✔	✤	✤	✤	✤	✔
VOCABULARY STRATEGIES																				
Decoding Multipart Words		✤		✔		✤						✤		✔		✤				
WORD-LEARNING STRATEGIES																				
Context Clues	✤	✤	✤	✤	✔	✤	✤	✤	✤	✔	✤	✤	✤	✤	✔	✤	✤	✤	✤	✔
Glossary Use	✤				✔	✤	✤	✤	✤	✔	✤	✤	✤	✤	✔	✤	✤	✤	✤	✔
Dictionary Use		✤				✤	✤	✤	✤	✔	✤	✤	✤	✤	✔	✤	✤	✤	✤	✔
Online-Dictionary Use			✤			✤	✤	✤	✤	✔	✤	✤	✤	✤	✔	✤	✤	✤	✤	✔
STRATEGY BOOKMARK						✻	✻	✻	✻	✔	✤	✤	✤	✤	✔	✤	✤	✤	✤	✔
HIGHER-ORDER THINKING																				
Bloom's Taxonomy/ Standardized-Test Practice		✔		✔			✔		✔			✔		✔			✔		✔	
Graphic Organizer	■	■	■	■	■	■	■	■		■	■	■	■	■	■	■	■	■	■	■
Metacognition	■	■	■	■	■	■	■	■	■	■	■	■	■	■	■	■	■	■	■	■
FLUENCY STRATEGIES																				
Oral Reading	✔		■	✔	✔			■		✔	✔			■	✔	✔			■	✔
Silent Reading		■	■					■	■				■	■				■	■	
DIFFERENTIATED INSTRUCTION/RESPONSE TO INTERVENTION																				
Strategies and Tips				■					■					■						■

✱ = Strong Teacher Support   ✻ = Moderate Teacher Support   ✤ = Student Independence   ■ = Practiced   ✔ = Knowledge/Evaluative Check

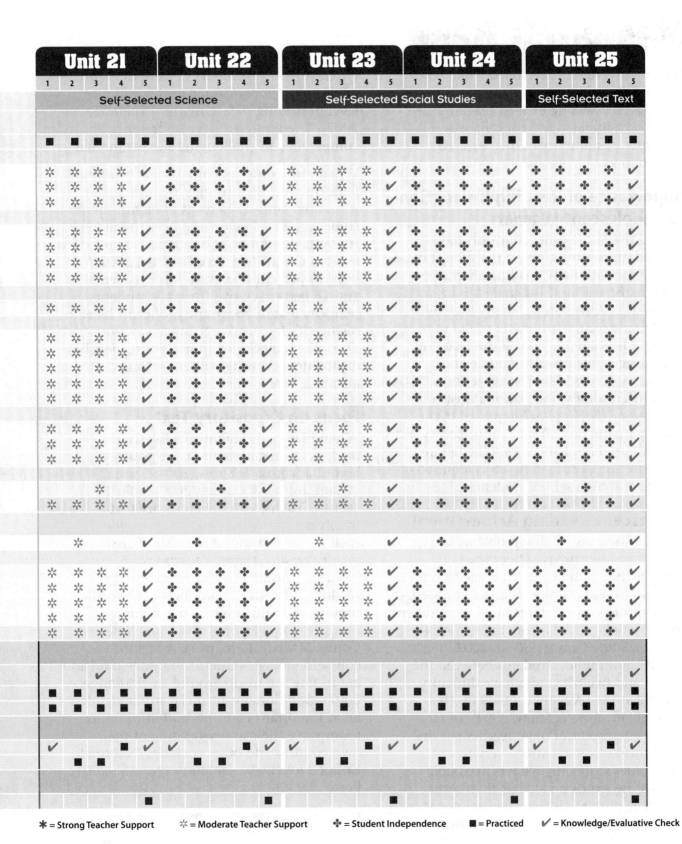

Unit 21	Unit 22	Unit 23	Unit 24	Unit 25
1 2 3 4 5	1 2 3 4 5	1 2 3 4 5	1 2 3 4 5	1 2 3 4 5
Self-Selected Science		Self-Selected Social Studies		Self-Selected Text

✹ = Strong Teacher Support   ✷ = Moderate Teacher Support   ❖ = Student Independence   ■ = Practiced   ✔ = Knowledge/Evaluative Check

Research Base

Read to Achieve was developed based on best practices and recommendations found in research assessing explicit teaching, adolescent literacy, and content-area literature. A summary of this research base follows.

Importance of Reading Instruction for Adolescent Learners

During the last decade, educators have focused much attention on the subject of reading; traditionally, reading on grade level by the end of third grade has been the goal. Unfortunately, "many excellent third-grade readers will falter or fail in later-grade academic tasks if the teaching of reading is neglected in middle and secondary grades" (Biancarosa & Snow, 2004, p. 1). Interestingly, the National Institute for Literacy (NIFL) (2007) reported that literacy instruction should continue beyond elementary school and should be tailored to the more complex reading tasks required of middle and high school students.

Adolescent Reading Achievement

"One of the most vexing problems facing middle and secondary school teachers today is that many students come into their classrooms without the requisite knowledge, skills, or disposition to read and comprehend the materials placed before them" (RAND Reading Study Group [RRSG], 2002, p. iii). About eight million students between the fourth and twelfth grades have difficulty reading at the level appropriate for their grade (Biancarosa & Snow, 2004). In fact, "some 70 percent of older readers require some form of remediation. Very few of these older struggling readers need help to read the words on a page; their most common problem is that they are not able to comprehend what they read" (Biancarosa & Snow, p. 3). Unfortunately, according to the 2007 National Assessment of Educational Progress (NAEP), only 31 percent of eighth-grade students performed at the proficient level in reading (Lee, Grigg, & Donahue, 2007). The proficient level represents competency in challenging subject matter.

When one examines content-area reading performance, the findings are indeed troubling. Only 17 percent of eighth-grade students and 13 percent of twelfth-grade students performed at or above the proficient level in U.S. history (Lee & Weiss, 2007); only 29 percent of eighth-grade students and 18 percent of twelfth-grade students performed at or above the proficient level in science (Grigg, Lauko, & Brockway, 2006). Thus, the majority of adolescent readers have difficulties accessing content-area text at adequate levels.

Focus on Expository Text

When reading is taught to adolescent readers, the focus should be expository text (Biancarosa & Snow, 2004; Lenski, Wham, Johns, & Caskey, 2007; NIFL, 2007; Sáenz & Fuchs, 2002). Expository text involves reading that *explains something,* such as the text found in content-area science or social studies textbooks. Science has a significant place in education. "In a world filled with the products of scientific inquiry, scientific literacy has become a necessity for everyone" (National Research Council [NRC], 1996, p. 1). A scientific education allows students to understand and appreciate the world around them (Rangel, 2007). Additionally, in social studies students learn important concepts and information to improve their understanding of their own country and other societies (National Council for the Social Studies [NCSS], 2001; Porter, 2006).

How Content-Area Text is Different

For a variety of reasons, adolescent learners struggle to read their content-area textbooks.

These students have fewer experiences reading these types of text (Lenski et al., 2007). Content-area material is also typically denser than narrative text (Coyne, Kame'enui, & Carnine, 2007), and the organization is often difficult to follow (Abadiano & Turner, 2002; Sáenz & Fuchs, 2002). Vocabulary tends to be much more technical (Abadiano & Turner; Ediger, 2002; Fang, 2006; Sáenz & Fuchs). Further, many students have difficulty even reading the more cumbersome multipart words often found in science and social studies textbooks (Fang). Clearly, more intentional instruction is warranted in the content areas. In fact, "numerous studies over the past few decades have demonstrated that it is most helpful to teach comprehension strategies, text structures, and word-level strategies while students are engaged in reading challenging, content-rich texts" (Heller & Greenleaf, 2007, p. 8).

The Importance of Explicit Instruction

"Given that students find expository reading more difficult than narrative reading, it is surprising that they are rarely given explicit instruction on how to read expository text" (Sáenz & Fuchs, 2002, p. 33). Explicit instruction involves direct teaching, including teacher modeling, guided student practice with feedback, and independent student practice (Hock, Deshler, & Schumaker, 2000; Marchand-Martella & Martella, 2009; NIFL, 2007). Biancarosa and Snow (2004) cited the importance of direct, explicit instruction in adolescent literacy programs. Kirschner, Sweller, and Clark (2006) found research "almost uniformly supports direct, strong instructional guidance" (p. 83). Interestingly, Klahr and Nigam (2004) compared the effectiveness of explicit instruction to discovery learning in a science class. They found more students learned science skills when explicit instruction was provided, compared to a discovery-based approach. In addition, those students who learned through explicit instruction displayed generalized knowledge

equivalent to those few students who learned through discovery.

Comprehension Strategies

"Comprehension is the essence of reading and the ultimate goal of reading instruction" (Vaughn & Bos, 2009), p. 312). Much research has examined the effectiveness of teaching comprehension strategies to students. In fact, "the effectiveness of teaching reading comprehension strategies has been the subject of over 500 studies in the last 25 years. The simple conclusion from this work is that strategy instruction improves comprehension" (Willingham, 2006/2007, p. 39). Phelps (2005) examined research involving adolescent literacy and concluded that strategy-based (strategic) instruction aids in better text understanding. When comprehension strategies are taught, readers become more "purposeful, strategic, and critical" (NIFL, 2007, p. 19). The following skills and strategies can be targeted for instruction in an adolescent literacy program: using text features, making text connections, identifying text structure, monitoring comprehension, using questioning and mnemonic strategies, and taking effective lecture notes (for details, see Lenski et al., 2007; Meltzer, Smith, & Clark, 2001).

Using text features. Textbooks have features such as titles and subheads, an index and a glossary, bold and highlighted words, visuals and their captions, and sidebars; these text features aid students in learning and remembering information (Lenski et al., 2007). The importance of using text features is supported in the literature (Boynton & Blevins, 2003; Lenski et al., 2007; Ogle & Blachowicz, 2002; Schoenbach, Greenleaf, Cziko, & Hurwitz, 1999). Students tend to have a better understanding of what is presented in the text when they are taught to preview and use these text features.

Making text connections. Text connections involve relating to or connecting with what is being read (Massey & Heafner, 2004). These connections help foster motivation and reading engagement (Lenski et al., 2007; Tovani, 2000). Making text connections in content-area materials can involve identifying the topic of what will be read (Duffy, 2003), establishing a purpose for reading (NIFL, 2007; Tovani, 2000), and activating prior or background knowledge about the topic (Carnine, Silbert, Kame'enui, & Tarver, 2004; Neufeld, 2005/2006). The importance of making text connections is supported in the literature (Barton, Heidema, & Jordan, 2002; Cottrell & McNamara, 2002; Schoenbach et al., 1999; Townsend & Clarihew, 1989; Vaughn & Bos, 2009).

Identifying text structure. Text structure refers to the way in which text is organized (Montelongo, Berber-Jiménez, Hernández, & Hosking, 2006; National Education Association [NEA], 2006). Types of text structure found in content-area text include description-or-list, order-or-sequence, cause-and-effect, and compare-and-contrast (NIFL, 2007). Authors use this text organization to communicate information to the reader. The importance of identifying text structure is supported in the literature (Bakken, Mastropieri, & Scruggs, 1997; Bakken & Whedon, 2002; Duke & Pearson, 2002; Gajria, Jitendra, Sood, & Sacks, 2007; Heller & Greenleaf, 2007; Lenski et al., 2007; Montelongo et al., 2006; NIFL, 2007). Explicit text-structure instruction is needed.

Monitoring comprehension. Comprehension monitoring refers to when students learn to determine what they do and don't understand and when they learn to use the appropriate strategies to improve their understanding (Armbruster, Lehr, & Osborn, 2003; Kamil, 2004; NIFL, 2007). Two ways students can improve their understanding through comprehension monitoring are slowing down when reading and rereading difficult text (Robb, 1995; Schoenbach et al., 1999). The importance of monitoring comprehension is supported in the literature (Biancarosa & Snow, 2004; NIFL, 2007; RRSG, 2002; Schoenbach et al., 1999).

Using questioning and mnemonic strategies. Questioning strategies involve having students develop questions based on what they're reading (Rosenshine, Meister, & Chapman, 1996; Vaughn & Bos, 2009). Students who generate questions are typically more motivated to read the text, to clarify information they don't know, and to exhibit inferential thinking (Tovani, 2000). Mnemonic strategies are memory devices that aid students in remembering and retrieving important information (Lenski et al., 2007; Mastropieri & Scruggs, 1996).

SQ3R is a questioning and mnemonic strategy used to assist students in learning information from content-area text. The SQ3R strategy is "probably the best-known technique for learning information from text" (Vaughn & Bos, 2009, p. 443). SQ3R stands for Survey, Question, Read, Reflect, and Review, although other Rs are noted (e.g., Recite). When students survey text, they scan the beginning, the main part, and the end of a chapter, examining titles and subheads, sidebars, and visuals with captions. Next, they develop questions and answers. Typically questions are developed from titles or subheads and bold and highlighted words; students learn to adjust their questions based on what they read. After students answer these questions, they reflect on their written notes, making important text-to-text, text-to-self, and text-to-world connections (Tovani, 2000). Finally, students review their written notes. This review serves as an important study strategy (Lenski et al., 2007).

Students can also use a questioning and mnemonic strategy called QHL to enhance comprehension of content-area material. QHL stands for "What *questions* do I have?", "*How* will I find the answers?", and "What did I *learn* after finding the answers?". The importance of questioning and mnemonic strategies is supported in the literature (Adams, Carnine, & Gersten, 1982; Chastain & Thurber, 1989; Hartlep & Forsyth, 2000; RRSG, 2002; Trabasso & Bouchard, 2002; Vaughn & Bos, 2009).

Lecture note taking. Note taking helps students record information presented in a lecture or a class discussion. The two-column note-taking strategy, also known as the Cornell method, works well when lecture information is presented in a "main ideas and details" format (Lenski et al., 2007), with main ideas in the left column and the corresponding details in the right column (Lenski et al.; Vaughn & Bos). Students then use these notes as a study guide (Ogle, 1996; Santa, Havens, & Harrison, 1996). The importance of lecture note taking is supported in the literature (Faber, Morris, & Lieberman, 2000; Heward, 2009; Lenski et al., 2007; Vaughn & Bos, 2009). Note taking allows for better understanding and recall of lecture information.

Vocabulary Strategies

"Vocabulary is the knowledge of words and word meanings" (Diamond & Gutlohn, 2006, p. 3). Vocabulary strategies are closely tied to reading comprehension (Graves & Fink, 2007). In fact, "one of the oldest findings in educational research is the strong relationship between vocabulary knowledge and reading comprehension" (Stahl, 1999, p. 3). Vocabulary knowledge is especially important in informational texts, such as science and social studies, where precise meanings are often central to understanding (Blachowicz, Fisher, Ogle, & Watts-Taffe, 2006). Most vocabulary is learned indirectly through daily language and reading opportunities; however, some vocabulary must be taught directly. The most effective vocabulary instruction includes the direct teaching of specific words and word-learning strategies (Armbruster et al., 2003; Vaughn & Bos, 2009). The following skills and strategies can be targeted for instruction in an adolescent literacy program: decoding multipart words (to read long words) and word-learning strategies such as context clues and reference aids (e.g., glossary, dictionary, or online dictionary) (to determine the words' meanings) (Lenski et al., 2007; Vaughn & Bos, 2009).

Decoding multipart words. Decoding multipart words is a strategy students can use to read longer and more difficult words before determining the words' meanings. Decoding multipart words is a flexible strategy that breaks words into smaller parts so they can be read more easily without using formal syllabication (Archer, Gleason, & Vachon, 2003). "The meaning of content-area passages is almost totally carried by the multisyllabic words" (Archer et al., p. 90). "Not surprisingly, the inability to decode multi-syllabic words negatively influences readers' comprehension" (NIFL, 2007, p. 5). The importance of learning to decode multisyllabic/multipart words is supported in the literature (Archer et al., 2003; Knight-McKenna, 2008; Vaughn & Bos, 2009).

Word-learning strategies. Specific-word instruction teaches individual words to students. "Of course, it is not possible for teachers to provide specific instruction for all the words their students do not know. Therefore, students . . . need to develop effective word-learning strategies" (Armbruster et al., 2003, p. 37). Word-learning strategies are ways of accessing word meaning in an independent manner; the strategies include the use of context clues and reference aids. Context clues involve defining unknown words using the surrounding words or sentences to derive their meaning (Carnine, Silbert, Kame'enui, Tarver, & Jungjohann, 2006; Edwards, Font, Baumann, & Boland, 2004). The importance of using context clues is supported in the literature (Diamond & Gutlohn, 2006; Duffy, 2003; Edwards et al., 2004; Fukkink & de Glopper, 1998; Lenski et al., 2007; Nagy, Herman, & Anderson, 1985).

Reference aids are helpful tools students use to determine word meaning (e.g., glossary, dictionary, or online dictionary) (Armbruster et al., 2003; Vaughn & Bos, 2009). The importance of using reference aids is supported in the literature (Beck, McKeown, & Kucan, 2002; Carnine et al., 2004; Carnine et al., 2006; Diamond & Gutlohn, 2006; Lehr,

Osborn, & Hiebert, 2003; RRSG, 2002; Scott & Nagy, 1997; Stahl, 1999). Using reference aids such as glossaries, dictionaries, and computer resources (an online dictionary) is a helpful word-learning strategy for finding the meaning of unknown words independently.

Fluency Strategies

Fluency is the ability to read text quickly, accurately, and with expression (Rasinski, 2004, 2006). The best method of improving reading fluency is through repeated oral reading (Hasbrouck, 2006; Hasbrouck & Tindal, 2006; Therrien, 2004). The importance of fluency practice is supported in the literature (Armbruster et al., 2003; O'Connor, White, & Swanson, 2007; RRSG, 2002; Rasinski, 2004, 2006; Rasinski et al., 2005; Samuels, Schermer, & Reinking, 1992; Vaughn & Bos, 2009). Rather than focusing on the decoding of words, students who read fluently are able to give greater attention to understanding the material and to using strategies they've learned.

Higher-Order Thinking

The development of higher-order thinking skills is promoted through questions and activities related to Bloom's Taxonomy (Anderson et al., 2001). Additionally, the use of visual aids such as graphic organizers improves reading comprehension, especially in the content areas (Kim, Vaughn, Wanzek, & Wei, 2004).

Bloom's Taxonomy. The Taxonomy of Educational Objectives was originated by Benjamin S. Bloom in 1956 and is commonly called Bloom's Taxonomy (Krathwohl, 2002). Bloom's Taxonomy was created to develop a common language regarding educational goals and to aid in the decision-making process regarding curriculum. More recently, the original taxonomy was revised (Anderson et al., 2001). The revised Bloom's Taxonomy divides cognitive processes into six categories: remembering, understanding, applying, analyzing, evaluating, and creating. These categories follow a continuum

from least complex to most complex. The importance of using a continuum of questions with particular focus on higher-order questions is supported in the literature (Anderson et al.; Heward, 2009; Lord & Baviskar, 2007; RRSG, 2002). Students should have increased experiences with questions to promote higher-order thinking skills.

Graphic organizers. Graphic organizers are visual aids that illustrate how ideas are connected or organized (Lenski et al., 2007). The importance of graphic organizers is supported in the literature (Boyle, 2000; DiCecco & Gleason, 2002; Harvey, 1998; Kamil, 2004; Kim et al., 2004; Lenz, Ellis, & Scanlon, 1996; NIFL, 2007; Trabasso & Bouchard, 2002; Vaughn & Bos, 2009). Graphic organizers facilitate the learning of more complex material.

Metacognition. "Metacognition is the awareness and regulation of one's thinking processes, that is, thinking about your thinking" (Klingner, Vaughn, Dimino, Schumm, & Bryant, 2001, p. 15). Students need to think about what comprehension strategies they're using and if these strategies are appropriate. The importance of metacognition is supported in the literature (Biancarosa & Snow, 2004; Carnine et al., 2004; Kamil, 2004; NIFL, 2007; Pressley, 2002; Schoenbach et al., 1999).

Summary

Read to Achieve is built on a solid foundation of effective skills and strategies in comprehension, vocabulary, and fluency building. Further, this program is age- and grade-appropriate for adolescent learners who require a different focus when it comes to reading instruction. These students need to be taught skills and strategies they'll ultimately use in authentic content-area text in other classes, they need to be given opportunities to develop higher-order thinking skills, and they need to receive text-based, collaborative-learning activities to promote problem-solving and metacognition.

References

Abadiano, H., & Turner, J. (2002). Reading expository text: The challenges of students with learning disabilities. *New England Reading Association Journal, 38,* 49–55.

Adams, A., Carnine, D., & Gersten, R. (1982). Instructional strategies for studying content area texts in the intermediate grades. *Reading Research Quarterly, 18,* 27–55.

Anderson, L. W., Krathwohl, D. R., Airasian, P. W., Cruikshank, K. A., Mayer, R. E., Pintrich, P. R., et al. (2001). *A taxonomy for learning, teaching, and assessing: A revision of Bloom's taxonomy of educational objectives.* New York: Longman.

Archer, A, L., Gleason, M. M., & Vachon, V. L. (2003). Decoding and fluency: Foundation skills for struggling older readers. *Learning Disability Quarterly, 26,* 89–101.

Armbruster, B. B., Lehr, F., & Osborn, J. (2003). *Put reading first: The research building blocks for teaching children to read* (2nd ed.). Jessup, MD: Center for the Improvement of Early Reading Achievement.

Bakken, J. P., Mastropieri, M. A., & Scruggs, T. E. (1997). Reading comprehension of expository science material and students with learning disabilities: A comparison of strategies. *The Journal of Special Education, 31,* 300–324.

Bakken, J. P., & Whedon, C. K. (2002). Teaching text structure to improve reading comprehension. *Intervention in School and Clinic, 37,* 229–233.

Barton, M. L., Heidema, C., & Jordan, D. (2002). Teaching reading in mathematics and science. *Educational Leadership, 60,* 24–28.

Beck, I. L., McKeown, M. G., & Kucan, L. (2002). *Bringing words to life: Robust vocabulary instruction.* New York: Guilford.

Biancarosa, G., & Snow, C. (2004). *Reading next: A vision for action and research in middle and high school literacy: A report to Carnegie Corporation of New York* (2nd ed.). Washington DC: Alliance For Excellent Education.

Blachowicz, C. L. Z., Fisher, P. J. L., Ogle, D., & Watts-Taffe, S. (2006). Theory and research into practice: Vocabulary: Questions from the classroom. *Reading Research Quarterly, 41,* 524–539.

Boyle, J. R. (2000). The effects of a Venn diagram strategy on the literal, inferential, and relational comprehension of students with mild disabilities. *Learning Disabilities: A Multidisciplinary Journal, 10,* 5–13.

Boynton, A., & Blevins, W. (2003). *Teaching students to read nonfiction.* New York: Scholastic.

Carnine, D. W., Silbert, J., Kame'enui, E. J., & Tarver, S. G. (2004). *Direct instruction reading* (4th ed.). Upper Saddle River, NJ: Pearson.

Carnine, D. W., Silbert, J., Kame'enui, E. J., Tarver, S. G., & Jungjohann, K. (2006). *Teaching struggling and at-risk readers: A direct instruction approach.* Upper Saddle River, NJ: Pearson.

Chastain, G., & Thurber, S. (1989). The SQ3R study technique enhances comprehension of an introductory psychology textbook. *Reading Improvement, 26,* 94–96.

Cottrell, K. G., & McNamara, D. S. (2002). *Cognitive precursors to science comprehension.* Retrieved April 1, 2008, from http://cognitivesciencesociety.org/ confproc/gmu02/final_ind_files/Cottrell_McNamara.pdf

Coyne, M. D., Kame'enui, E. J., & Carnine, D. W. (2007). *Effective teaching strategies that accommodate diverse learners* (3rd ed.). Upper Saddle River, NJ: Prentice-Hall.

Diamond, L., & Gutlohn, L. (2006). *Vocabulary handbook.* Berkeley, CA: Consortium on Reading Excellence.

DiCecco, V. M., & Gleason, M. M. (2002). Using graphic organizers to attain relational knowledge from expository text. *Journal of Learning Disabilities, 35,* 306–320.

Duffy, G. G. (2003). *Explaining reading: A resource for teaching concepts, skills, and strategies.* New York: Guilford Press.

Duke, N. K., & Pearson, P. D. (2002). Effective practices for developing reading comprehension. In A. E. Farstrup & S. J. Samuels (Eds.), *What research has to say about reading instruction* (3rd ed.) (pp.205–242). Newark, DE: International Reading Association.

Ediger, M. (2002). Factors which make expository reading difficult. *Journal of Instructional Psychology, 29,* 312–316.

Edwards, E. C., Font, G., Baumann, J. F., & Boland, E. (2004). Unlocking word meanings: Strategies and guidelines for teaching morphemic and contextual analysis. In J. F. Baumann & E. J. Kame'enui (Eds.), *Vocabulary instruction: Research to practice* (pp. 159–176). New York: Guilford.

Faber, J. E., Morris, J. D., & Lieberman, M. G. (2000). The effect of note taking on ninth grade students' comprehension. *Reading Psychology, 21,* 257–270.

Fang, Z. (2006). The language demands of science reading in middle school. *International Journal of Science Education, 28,* 491–520.

Fukkink, R. G., & de Glopper, K. (1998). Effects of instruction in deriving word meaning from context: A meta–analysis. *Review of Educational Research, 68,* 450–469.

Gajria, M., Jitendra, A. K., Sood, S., & Sacks, G. (2007). Improving comprehension of expository text in students with LD: A research synthesis. *Journal of Learning Disabilities, 40,* 210–225.

Graves, M. F., & Fink, L. S. (2007). Vocabulary instruction in the middle grades. *Voices for the Middle, 15,* 13–19.

Grigg, W., Lauko, M., & Brockway, D. (2006). *The nation's report card: Science 2006* (NCES 2006–466). U.S. Department of Education, National Center for Education Statistics. Washington, DC: U.S. Government Printing Office.

Hasbrouck, J. (2006, Summer). Drop everything and read—but how? *American Educator, 22–31,* 46–47.

Hasbrouck, J., & Tindal, G. (2006). Oral reading fluency norms: A valuable assessment tool for reading teachers. *The Reading Teacher, 59,* 636–644.

Hartlep, K. L., & Forsyth, G. A. (2000). The effect of self-reference on learning and retention. *Teaching of Psychology, 27,* 269–271.

Harvey, S. (1998). *Nonfiction matters: Reading, writing, and research in grades 3–8.* York, ME: Stenhouse.

Heller, R., & Greenleaf, C. (2007). Literacy instruction in the content areas: Getting to the core of middle and high school improvement. Washington, DC: Alliance for Excellent Education.

Heward, W. L. (2009). *Exceptional students* (9th ed.). Upper Saddle River, NJ: Pearson.

Hock, M. F., Deshler, D. D., & Schumaker, J. B. (2000). *Strategic tutoring.* Lawrence, KS: Edge Enterprises.

Kamil, M. (2004). Vocabulary and comprehension instruction: Summary and implications of the National Reading Panel findings. In P. McCardle & V. Chhabra (Eds.), *The voice of evidence in reading research* (pp. 213–234). Baltimore: Brookes.

Kim, A., Vaughn, S., Wanzek, J., & Wei, S. (2004). Graphic organizers and their effects on the reading comprehension of students with LD: A synthesis of research. *Journal of Learning Disabilities, 37,* 105–118.

Kirschner, P. A., Sweller, J., & Clark, R. E. (2006). Why minimal guidance during instruction does not work: An analysis of the failure of constructivist, discovery, problem-based, experiential, and inquiry-based teaching. *Educational Psychologist, 41,* 75–86.

Klahr, D., & Nigam, M. (2004). The equivalence of learning paths in early science instruction: Effects of direct instruction and discovery learning. *Psychological Science, 15,* 661–667.

Klingner, J. K., Vaughn, S., Dimino, J., Schumm, J. S., & Bryant, D. (2001). *Collaborative strategic reading: Strategies for improving comprehension.* Longmont, CO: Sopris West.

Knight-McKenna, M. (2008). Syllable types: A strategy for reading multisyllabic words. *Teaching Exceptional Children, 40*(3), 18–24.

Krathwohl, D. R. (2002). A revision of Bloom's Taxonomy: An overview. *Theory Into Practice, 41,* 212–218.

Lee. J., Grigg, W., & Donahue, P. (2007). *The nation's report card: Reading 2007* (NCES 2007–496). U.S. Department of Education, National Center for Education Statistics, Washington, DC: U.S. Government Printing Office.

Lee, J., & Weiss, A. (2007). *The nation's report card. U.S. History 2006* (NCES 2007–474). U.S. Department of Education, National Center for Education Statistics. Washington, DC: U.S. Government Printing Office.

Lehr, F., Osborn, J., & Hiebert, E. H. (2003). *A focus on vocabulary.* Honolulu, HI: Pacific Resources for Education and Learning.

Lenski, S. D., Wham, M. A., Johns, J. L., & Caskey, M. M. (2007). *Reading and learning strategies: Middle grades through high school* (3rd ed.). Dubuque, IA: Kendall/Hunt.

Lenz, B. K., Ellis, E. S., & Scanlon, D. (1996). *Teaching learning strategies to adolescents and adults with learning disabilities.* Austin, TX: PRO-ED.

Lord, T., & Baviskar, S. (2007, March/April). Moving students from information recitation to information understanding: Exploiting Bloom's Taxonomy in creating science questions. *Journal of College Science Teaching,* 40–44.

Marchand-Martella, N. E., & Martella, R. C. (2009). Explicit instruction. In W. L. Heward (Ed.), *Exceptional children* (9th ed.) (pp. 196–198). Columbus, OH: Pearson/Merrill.

Massey, D. D., & Heafner, T. L. (2004). Promoting reading comprehension in social studies. *Journal of Adolescent & Adult Literacy, 48,* 26–40.

Mastropieri, M. A., & Scruggs, T. E. (1996). Reflections on "promoting thinking skills of students with learning disabilities: Effects on recall and comprehension of expository prose." *Exceptionality, 6,* 53–57.

Meltzer, J., Smith, N. C., & Clark, H. (2001). *Adolescent literacy resources: Linking research and practice.* Providence, RI: Northeast and Islands Regional Educational Laboratory at Brown University.

Montelongo, J., Berber-Jiménez, L., Hernández, A. C., & Hosking, D. (2006). Teaching expository text structures. *The Science Teacher, 73,* 28–31.

Nagy, W. E., Herman, P. A., & Anderson, R. C. (1985). Learning words from context. *Reading Research Quarterly, 20,* 233–253.

National Council for the Social Studies (NCSS). (2001). *Creating effective citizens.* Retrieved January 2, 2008, from http://www.socialstudies.org/positions/effectivecitizens/

National Education Association (NEA). (2006). *Using text structure.* Retrieved September 9, 2007, from http://www.nea.org/reading/usingtextstructure.html

National Institute for Literacy (NIFL). (2007). *What content-area teachers should know about adolescent literacy.* Retrieved February, 13, 2008, from http://www.nifl.gov/nifl/publications/adolescent_literacy07.pdf

National Research Council (NRC). (1996). *National science education standards.* Washington, DC: National Academy Press.

Neufeld, P. (2005/2006). Comprehension instruction in content area classes. *The Reading Teacher, 59,* 302–312.

O'Connor, R. E., White, A., & Swanson, H. L. (2007). Repeated reading versus continuous reading: Influences on reading fluency and comprehension. *Exceptional Children, 74,* 31–46.

Ogle, D. M. (1996). Study techniques that ensure content area reading success. In D. Lapp, J. Flood, & N. Farnan (Eds.), *Content area reading and learning instructional strategies* (2nd ed.) (pp. 3–14). Needham Heights, MA: Simon & Schuster.

Ogle, D., & Blachowicz, C. L. Z. (2002). Beyond literature circles: Helping students comprehend informational texts. In C. C. Block & M. Pressley (Eds.), *Comprehension instruction research-based best practices* (pp. 259–288). New York: Guilford.

Phelps, S. (2005). *Ten years of research on adolescent literacy, 1994–2004: A review.* Naperville, IL: Learning Point Associates.

Porter, P. (2006). Top ten reasons to include social studies in your instructional day. *Social Studies Review, 46,* 73–76.

Pressley, M. (2002). Metacognition and self-regulated comprehension. In A. E. Farstrup & S. J. Samuels (Eds.), *What research has to say about reading instruction* (3rd ed.) (pp. 205–242). Newark, DE: International Reading Association.

RAND Reading Study Group (RRSG). (2002). *Reading for understanding: Toward an R&D program in reading comprehension.* Washington, DC: RAND.

Rangel, E. S. (2007). Science education that makes sense. *Research Points, 5,* 1–4.

Rasinski, T. V. (2004). *Assessing reading fluency.* Honolulu, HI: Pacific Resources for Education and Learning.

Rasinski, T. V. (2006). Reading fluency instruction: Moving beyond accuracy, automaticity, and prosody. *The Reading Teacher, 59,* 704–706.

Rasinski, T. V., Padak, N. D., McKeon, C. A., Wilfong, L. G., Friedauer, J. A., & Heim, P. (2005). Is reading fluency a key for successful high school reading? *Journal of Adolescent & Adult Literacy, 49,* 22–27.

Robb, L. (1995). *Reading strategies that work: Teaching your students to become better readers.* New York: Scholastic.

Rosenshine, B., Meister, C., & Chapman, S. (1996). Teaching students to generate questions: A review of the intervention studies. *Review of Educational Research, 66,* 181–221.

Sáenz, L. M., & Fuchs, L. S. (2002). Examining the reading difficulty of secondary students with learning disabilities: Expository versus narrative text. *Remedial and Special Education, 23,* 31–41.

Samuels, S. J., Schermer, N., & Reinking, D. (1992). Reading fluency: Techniques for making decoding automatic. In S. J. Samuels & A. E. Farstrup (Eds.), *What research has to say about reading instruction* (pp. 124–144). Newark, DE: International Reading Association.

Santa, C. M., Havens, L., & Harrison, S. (1996). Teaching secondary science through reading, writing, studying, and problem solving. In D. Lapp, J. Flood, & N. Farnan (Eds.), *Content area reading and learning instructional strategies* (2nd ed.) (pp. 3–14). Needham Heights, MA: Simon & Schuster.

Schoenbach, R., Greenleaf, C., Cziko, C., & Hurwitz, L. (1999). *Reading for understanding: A guide to improving reading in middle and high school classrooms.* San Francisco, CA: Jossey-Bass.

Scott, J. A., & Nagy, W. E. (1997). Understanding the definitions of unfamiliar verbs. *Reading Research Quarterly, 32,* 184–200.

Stahl, S. A. (1999). *Vocabulary development.* Brookline, MA: Brookline Books.

Therrien, W. J. (2004). Fluency and comprehension gains as a result of repeated reading: A meta-analysis. *Remedial and Special Education, 25,* 252–261.

Tovani, C. (2000). *I read it, but I don't get it: Comprehension strategies for adolescent readers.* Portland, ME: Stenhouse.

Townsend, M. A. R., & Clarihew, A. (1989). Facilitating children's comprehension through the use of advanced organizers. *Journal of Reading Behavior, 21,* 15–35.

Trabasso, T., & Bouchard, E. (2002). Teaching readers how to comprehend text strategically. In C. C. Block & M. Pressley (Eds.), *Comprehension instruction: Research-based best practices.* New York: Guilford.

Vaughn, S., & Bos, C. S. (2009). *Strategies for teaching students with learning and behavior problems* (7th ed.). Upper Saddle River, NJ: Pearson.

Willingham, D. T. (2006/2007). The usefulness of brief instruction in reading comprehension strategies. *American Educator, 30,* 39–50.

Teaching Techniques

Read to Achieve can be used in whole-class instruction or with small groups. This section summarizes teaching techniques.

Setup and Program Introduction

Room arrangement isn't a critical factor in this program, given that both whole-class and partner-based activities are conducted. Therefore, students may sit at either desks or tables. Students should be able to see the board, overhead transparencies, or an LCD-projected computer screen (for use with the ePresentation CD-ROM).

A few additional student materials are also needed. Students will complete fluency timings twice in each unit; thus, they will need **colored pens** (one blue, one red) for charting their timings in their Workbook, as well as some type of **timing device** (a stopwatch or a kitchen timer). Beginning in Unit 17, students write on **notebook paper** as they take lecture notes. Beginning in Unit 18, most Workbook activities are completed on notebook paper as well. Students use the Content Reader and Workbook for the first twenty units of the program, but, beginning in Unit 21, students should have access to **classroom science and social studies textbooks** you select. To promote maximum success after the program is completed, the textbooks should preferably be those books used in the students' own science and social studies classes.

(**NOTE:** Beginning in Unit 21, students should ideally work from the same classroom science or social studies textbooks. However, in situations in which students have different textbooks, assign student partners who have the same textbooks; instruct students to complete activities on their own and then to discuss with their partners what they did. If no two students are working from the same classroom textbook, when students are finished with self-completed activities on their textbook section, you might instruct students to explain to other students what they did, as a "debriefing" activity. Of course, you will need to develop separate generalization activities for these students; for example, your prepared lectures should be based on the particular topic covered in each classroom textbook used.)

Read to Achieve includes many opportunities for partner-based activities. You should assign partners to ensure maximum on-task behavior rather than let students choose their own partners. You may keep the same partners throughout a lesson or vary them, depending on students' needs. Lessons take forty-five to fifty minutes to complete and may be carried over to an additional session or day. To achieve maximum effectiveness, conduct lessons five days per week; this schedule aligns to one lesson per day, or one unit per week, with the fifth lesson of every unit typically serving as a unit-assessment day. A fun, partner-based "think-pair-share" activity is also on the final day of the unit.

It is helpful to develop a set of expectations for the students before the program begins. These expectations tell students which behaviors you expect from them as they complete lessons. The acronym ACES may be used (*Attend* to the teacher, *Collaborate* with your partner, *Express* yourself through thoughtful comments and questions, and *Show* your best work). These expectations should be discussed, modeled, and practiced as necessary. Posting the expectations may serve as a helpful reminder of which behaviors you want to see. You can tell the students the word *ACES* relates to being "top notch," and those who follow ACES will be well on their way to learning important skills they'll use throughout their school careers.

Following Routines

Skills and strategies taught in **Read to Achieve** appear in routines (text in boxes with green titles). These routines provide suggested wording on what you should say and do in the program, as well as what students should say and do. Following the routines in the program will help ensure consistency across classrooms and students. These routines make it easier for you to do what you do best—*teach*—rather than spend time trying to plan and write lessons. Less work for you means more focused instruction for your students! The wording found in routines changes over time; more focused, teacher-directed routines occur when a skill or strategy is first taught, and more concise, student-directed routines occur when a skill or strategy has been practiced many times. The following activity from Unit 6, Lesson 1, is a typical activity and routine in **Read to Achieve**; the activity is labeled for your convenience.

Activity title •

Teacher-support bar
(red highlight indicates how much
support the teacher should provide
to students) •

Indicates what the teacher says •

Indicates what the teacher does •

Routine box (gives step-by-step
instructions for teaching a
skill or strategy) •

Indicates what students say •

Activity	TEACHER SUPPORT		
	STRONG	MODERATE	STUDENT INDEPENDENCE

Comprehension Monitoring

1. When you're reading a section or paragraph in your textbook, you may not understand everything you're reading. The topic may be confusing, or the vocabulary may be difficult. Sometimes there is so much information that it's hard to understand what you read. What do you do when you don't understand something you're reading? **Accept** reasonable responses.

2. Today you'll learn a strategy to help you fix problems while you're reading. This strategy is rereading and adjusting your reading rate.

3. When you reread and adjust your reading rate, you read a section or paragraph a second time, but you read it slower. Reading at a slower rate allows you to understand better the section or the paragraph you're reading. This strategy helps you have better comprehension.

4. [CR] **Direct** students to **Content Reader** page 72: *Cnidarians*, paragraph 1.

ROUTINE • Rereading and Adjusting Reading Rate

a. I'll reread and adjust my reading rate for this paragraph and think about what I'm reading.

b. **Model** think-aloud for rereading and adjusting rate.

Think-Aloud **Read Content Reader** paragraph 1 aloud at a fast rate. I just read this paragraph, but I'm unsure what this paragraph is really about. I need to reread this paragraph much slower so I can think about what I'm reading. **Read** paragraph 1 aloud at a slower rate, pausing after each sentence. Now I understand more about cnidarians because I slowed down and thought about what I was reading. ❖

5. What did you learn about cnidarians after I reread the paragraph slower? Ideas: *They are transparent. They have a central opening and tentacles like a jellyfish.*

6. When could you reread and adjust your reading rate? **Accept** reasonable responses.

7. Why should you reread and adjust your reading rate? **Accept** reasonable responses.

Teacher's Edition: Unit 6, Lesson 1

Professional Development Guide

Group and Individual Response

Some routines in **Read to Achieve** require group responses, and some require individual responses. Group responses are noted in pink text (e.g., *Classifying organisms*); these responses are singular words or phrases that require specific wording. For individual responses that don't require exact wording, you'll see the phrase *Accept reasonable responses,* or you'll again see pink text following the word *Idea(s)* (e.g., Idea: *D̲e̲m/o̲/cra̲/cy̲*), which indicates a suggested response.

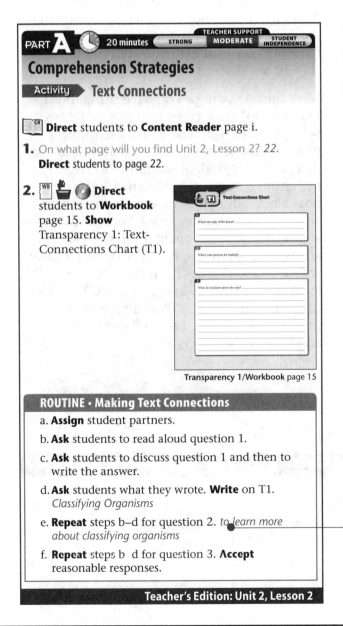

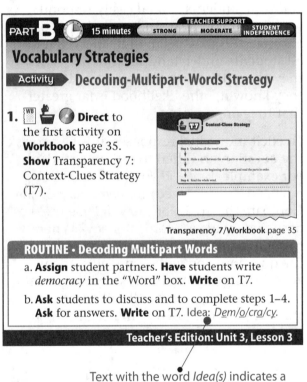

Text with the word *Idea(s)* indicates a suggested group response

Text without *Idea(s)* indicates an exact response from individual students

To elicit group responses, you may need to "signal" your students to respond together. One way to signal is to use voice inflection on the last word you say (e.g., What did you write for Question 1? with inflection on *1*). This added inflection serves as a cue for students to respond together. You can also add the words *everybody* or *everyone* to the end of your question (e.g., What did you write for Question 1, everybody?). You may choose to use audible signals, such as snapping your finger or tapping a pencil at the end of your question (e.g., What did you write for Question 1? [Snap.]). Whichever signal you choose, you should feel comfortable with the signal, *and* your students should easily respond together. If you hear students echoing one another, this may be an indication that not all students understand what to do. When they all respond together and "say it like they know it," the likelihood is far greater that they are learning.

To elicit individual responses, it is best to ask the question and then to call on a student. For example, How did you use the decoding-multipart-words strategy for *democracy*, Shane? Compare this to Shane, how did you use the decoding-multipart-words strategy? When the student's name is placed at the end of the question, you will ensure all students are listening and are on task, waiting for the name of the student you'll call on; if the student's name is used at the beginning of the question, other students may "tune out."

Corrections

No matter how well you provide instruction, all students make mistakes from time to time. Mistakes tell you important information about where students are having difficulties and where further instruction may be needed. If mistakes do occur, you'll typically see them during strong to moderate teacher support because students are first acquiring the skill or strategy. Fewer mistakes will occur as students become more accurate and fluent in their responding. During student independence, particularly during the unit preceding weekly review, few, if any, mistakes should occur. As skills and strategies are reviewed over time to ensure skill maintenance and generalization, you rarely should see student mistakes.

Most mistakes can be corrected using the "I Do, You Do" error-correction procedure (see below). When you hear a mistake during a group response, it is best not to draw attention to a particular student but rather to correct the entire group. Try to remain as positive as possible. Leading the students to the correct answer is not recommended, because this takes a great deal of time, could result in further errors, and does not ensure the correct answer will be found during the initial stages of learning (acquisition and accuracy). Therefore, the most efficient way of dealing with a mistake is to pinpoint the difficulty directly and fix it without negativity.

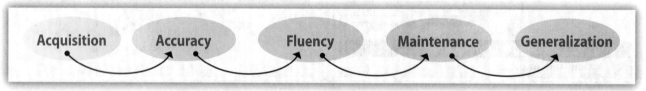

Steps	What Teacher Says/Does	What Students Say/Do
I do	Watch/listen as I show you _____. State the question, and say the answer. Add emphasis to the answer. Provide justification, if warranted.	Watch or listen.
You do	Restate the question.	Provide the correct response.

For example, in Unit 3, Lesson 3 (at right), suppose the teacher asks the students what they wrote for Question 2 on the Text-Connections Chart and she hears a mistake. She should say, Listen as I show you. Your purpose for reading is *to learn more about the rise of democracy* ("I do"), emphasizing the key words in the answer. She then should restate the question: So what's your purpose for reading? This gives the students an opportunity to provide the correct answer ("You do"). Following this student response, the teacher should tell the students to write the correct answer, if they haven't already done so. If students do not respond together, or if they echo one another, you can tell them you need to hear everyone together. Then repeat the question. This ensures students are paying attention and are firm in their responses.

When you hear an incorrect individual response, you should provide an "I do" and then ask the "You do" of the group, again trying not to draw attention to any particular student. For example, in Unit 7, Lesson 2 (on the next page), suppose the teacher calls on a student pair to ask how they defined the word *tertiary* using the Content Reader glossary, and the students say, *Third,* rather than the correct *Third level*. The teacher should say, Listen as I show you. The definition of *tertiary* is "third level" ("I do"), emphasizing the missing word in the definition. She should continue, providing a justification: We have to be sure to get the complete glossary definition so we know the word's full meaning. The teacher should then ask the group the definition of *tertiary*; after they respond, she should write the full definition on the transparency ("You do"). The teacher should tell students to write the definition in their Workbook, if they haven't already done so. If you find a student "shutting down" when a mistake is corrected, even when the correction is delivered to a group, you may try validating the attempt (e.g., That was a good try. Part of the definition of *tertiary* is "third." Then follow the "I Do, You Do" error-correction procedure).

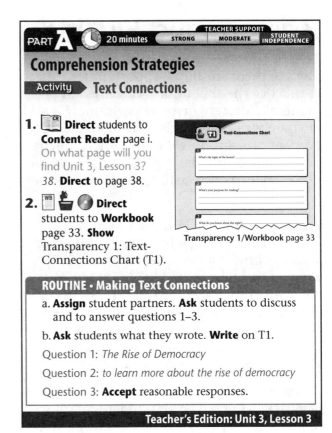

Transparency 1/Workbook page 33

ROUTINE · Making Text Connections

a. **Assign** student partners. **Ask** students to discuss and to answer questions 1–3.

b. **Ask** students what they wrote. **Write** on T1.

Question 1: *The Rise of Democracy*

Question 2: *to learn more about the rise of democracy*

Question 3: **Accept** reasonable responses.

Teacher's Edition: Unit 3, Lesson 3

As your students become more independent in their use of a skill or strategy (moving from fluency to generalization), you may lead the students to the answer because at this point they are more likely to produce the right answer quickly (e.g., Take a look at the definition of *tertiary,* and tell me if it is a complete one), or you may ask other students if they agree with the response. You might ask students to raise their hands or thumbs when they hear an incorrect response. For example, in Unit 3, Lesson 4 (on the next page), suppose the teacher calls on a student pair to ask how they used the context-clues strategy for *triumvirate,* and the students take turns telling what they did, but they define *triumvirate* incompletely as "a government." The teacher should say, Does everyone agree with this definition? and then should call on another pair of students to provide the full answer: *A government of three people with equal power. Caesar, Pompey, and Crassus formed a triumvirate.* The teacher should tell students to write the definition, if they haven't already done so.

Mastery and Firming

Read to Achieve is structured to ensure student success; there are ample opportunities to practice the skill until it is learned or mastered. Mastery involves performing a skill or strategy at high levels. You should make every effort—by closely monitoring student performance and making adjustments when necessary—to ensure student mastery in the program.

Mastery is enhanced through firming. Firming is repeating a part of a routine that students find troublesome. For example, suppose in a Glossary Use activity, students have difficulty using the Content Reader glossary. The teacher should provide an error correction and then might have students look up and define another word in the glossary to ensure "firm" responding.

This repetition, and your careful and focused feedback, will help ensure student mastery of a skill or strategy. If you hear one or more students responding in a tentative manner, it is best to firm that part of the routine before moving on. This will take extra time, but, in the long run, students will make fewer mistakes, will maintain higher performance levels, and will more likely exhibit generalized performance in novel situations. When in doubt, repeat the troublesome part of the routine until firm.

Pacing

Active student engagement is enhanced when teachers maintain a brisk pace while teaching. In doing so, teachers cover more material, which allows students to learn more material. When pacing is slow and labored, students lose interest, which is associated with decreased student involvement, lower achievement, and behavior problems. You'll know if your pacing is too fast or too slow by how well your students are performing: If they are engaged and participating at high levels, your pacing is probably on the mark; if your students are inattentive, are off task, or struggle with lesson content, you may need to adjust your pacing.

Student Motivation and Validation

Teachers play a key role in student motivation. By simply teaching a lesson that students achieve success in learning is motivating in and of itself. Allowing students

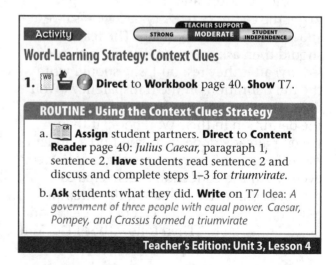

Activity | TEACHER SUPPORT | STRONG | MODERATE | STUDENT INDEPENDENCE

Word-Learning Strategy: Glossary Use

1. Direct students to **Content Reader** page 260.

2. **Direct** students to the second activity on **Workbook** page 91. **Show** T11.

ROUTINE • Using a Glossary

a. **Assign** student partners.

b. **Ask** students what letter the word will be under in the glossary. *T.*

c. **Have** students find *tertiary* and its definition in the glossary.

d. **Ask** students to discuss and then to write the definition in the "Glossary Definition" box. **Monitor** students. **Guide** as needed.

e. **Ask** students what they wrote. **Write** on T11. *Third-level*

Teacher's Edition: Unit 7, Lesson 2

Activity | TEACHER SUPPORT | STRONG | MODERATE | STUDENT INDEPENDENCE

Word-Learning Strategy: Context Clues

1. **Direct** to **Workbook** page 40. **Show** T7.

ROUTINE • Using the Context-Clues Strategy

a. **Assign** student partners. **Direct** to **Content Reader** page 40: *Julius Caesar,* paragraph 1, sentence 2. **Have** students read sentence 2 and discuss and complete steps 1–3 for *triumvirate.*

b. **Ask** students what they did. **Write** on T7 Idea: *A government of three people with equal power. Caesar, Pompey, and Crassus formed a triumvirate*

Teacher's Edition: Unit 3, Lesson 4

to collaborate with a partner also enhances student interest; students collaborate with a partner for almost every activity in **Read to Achieve,** from units including moderate

teacher support to those with student independence and then review activities. Further, every fifth lesson in **Read to Achieve** includes a think-pair-share strategy activity, such as the one for Unit 16, Lesson 5, below left.

Teachers can also comment on or validate their students' success. This validation has often been called "catching students being good." Student validation is easy to provide. For example, after a correct response, you can say Yes and then repeat what students say. Suppose in Unit 4, Lesson 2 (see below), you ask students, Why did you choose the Compare-and-Contrast Chart? and they respond, *The paragraphs tell how Ptolemy's and Copernicus's beliefs about the universe were different. Compare-and-Contrast tells how things are the same and how they're different.* You could validate them by saying, Yes. The paragraphs do tell how Ptolemy's and Copernicus's beliefs about the universe were different. Compare-and-Contrast tells how things are the same and how they're different. This type of validation gives specific feedback to students about their response. General statements, such as "super," "great," or "good job," can also be rewarding to students; however, they do not provide specific feedback.

PART B 🕐 15 minutes | STRONG | TEACHER SUPPORT MODERATE | STUDENT INDEPENDENCE

Higher-Order Thinking Skills

Activity ▶ **Think-Pair-Share Strategy**

Bloom's Taxonomy ▲

1. 📕 **Direct** students to **Content Reader** page 206. You're going to use the think-pair-share strategy to extend your learning about what the culture of the 1950s was like in the United States.

2. 📒💿 **Direct** students to **Workbook** page 256.

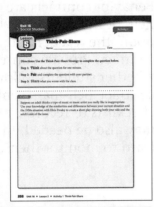

ROUTINE · Using the Think-Pair-Share Strategy

a. **Assign** student partners.

b. **Call** on students to read steps 1–3.

c. **Call** on a student to read the "Create" question. *Suppose an adult thinks a type of music or music artist you really like is inappropriate. Use your knowledge of the similarities and differences between your current situation and the 1950s situation with Elvis Presley to create a short play showing both your side and the adult's side of the issue.*

d. **Allow** one minute for think time.

e. **Call** on students to talk about what they were thinking. Ideas: *How 1950s images made it look like children were well behaved and maybe didn't argue much with their parents. How parents thought Elvis Presley acted inappropriately when he performed, just as my parents think some of the bands I listen to act inappropriately when they perform.*

f. **Have** students work with their partners for five minutes to share ideas and to answer the question. **Have** students write in their own **Workbook.**

g. **Call** on students to share their answers. **Accept** reasonable responses.

Teacher's Edition: Unit 16, Lesson 5

ROUTINE · Identifying Text Structure: Compare-and-Contrast

a. **Assign** student partners.

b. **Ask** students to identify and to discuss the most fitting type of text structure.

c. **Ask** students which text structure they chose. *Compare-and-Contrast.*

d. **Ask** students to discuss why they chose Compare-and-Contrast.

e. **Ask** students why they chose Compare-and-Contrast. Ideas: *The paragraphs tell how Ptolemy's and Copernicus's beliefs about the universe were different. Compare-and-Contrast tells how things are the same and how they're different.*

f. **Ask** students to discuss why the other types of text structure didn't fit these paragraphs.

Teacher's Edition: Unit 4, Lesson 2

Behavior Management

Management problems should be seen as an opportunity to instruct students how to behave more appropriately in the classroom. Telling students what they are doing (e.g., You're talking to your neighbor), what they need to do (e.g., You need to get back to work), and then validating the new behavior when it is shown (e.g., Thanks for working quietly) is a relatively easy way to ensure better behavior in the classroom.

Remember, ACES may be used to ensure better student behavior (see Setup and Program Introduction on page 31). Teach these expectations to your students, and "catch students being good" when they exhibit these behaviors (e.g., Great job collaborating with your partner, Malcolm). ACES also allows you to prompt for better behavior (e.g., You should be collaborating with your partner, Anita). Again, posting these expectations may serve as a helpful reminder to students of what behaviors you want to see.

If these basic strategies are not working with one or more of your students, you may need to implement a point system or a behavior contract. Point systems are structured so students earn points for good behavior and do not earn points when classroom expectations are not followed. Try to avoid removing points that have already been earned.

Behavior contracts are developed with the help of the student. When terms are agreed upon, the teacher and the student sign the contract. Provide consequences based on whether students follow the terms of the contract. Self-management strategies, such as checklists or recording or monitoring forms, may also be needed. In this way, students learn to monitor their own behavior.

Differentiated Instruction

Differentiated instruction means teaching to students' individual needs rather than applying one method to an entire class. *Read to Achieve* includes two types of differentiated instruction and Response to Intervention. First, the very structure of the program allows teachers to provide as much of the program as needed to teach the skills and strategies necessary for success in content-area classes (see Lesson Acceleration and Remediation on this page). Second, beginning in Unit 2, on the last page of every fifth lesson in the Teacher's Edition, you'll find recommendations for differentiating instruction (Response to Intervention) aligned with assessment performance.

As you can see in the example on the next page, differentiated instruction/Response to Intervention in Unit 4 is aligned to the Unit 4 Assessment; instructional recommendations are provided based on the learner's performance. Recommendations for students approaching mastery, students at mastery, and ELL students are given through Unit 25 to ensure student success in (and eventually out of) the program.

Lesson Acceleration and Remediation

Based on the foundational premise of differentiated instruction, *Read to Achieve* can be used with students across grade and skill levels. The chart on page 41 provides recommendations for which units can be taught to students in general education who are above grade level, those in general education who are below grade level, and students who are in reading-intervention classes or who receive support through special-education services. When in doubt about a student's skill level, administer the Placement Test (in Appendix B of this guide).

Analyze Unit 4 Assessment Results

Differentiated Instruction

Points Scored for Part A

5 or fewer points = **Approaching Mastery**

6 points = **At Mastery**

5 or fewer points = **ELL**

Approaching Mastery	At Mastery	ELL
• **Pair** student with "at mastery" student to review Text-Connections Chart (T1); have student make test corrections. • **Review** until firm Text-Connections Chart (T1) (see **Teacher's Edition** Unit 1, Lessons 1–4, Part A); have student make test corrections.	• **Assign** student to "be the teacher," partnering with "approaching mastery" or ELL student to review Text-Connections Chart (T1). • **Assign** student to research one or more topics covered in **Content Reader** Unit 4; have student make test corrections.	• **Provide** guided notes (partially completed Text-Connections Chart [T1]), and help student fill in missing words; assist with test corrections; retest missed items. • **Provide** verbal scaffolding to encourage student to use Text-Connections Chart (T1); assist with test corrections; retest missed items.

Points Scored for Part B

7 or fewer points = **Approaching Mastery**

8 points = **At Mastery**

7 or fewer points = **ELL**

Approaching Mastery	At Mastery	ELL
• **Review** until firm text structure (see **Teacher's Edition** Units 2 and 3, Lessons 1–4, Part A: Text Structure); have student make test corrections. • **Provide** written prompt describing four text-structure types; have student make test corrections.	• **Direct** student to alternate content-specific materials (e.g., magazines, newspapers, Internet). • **Direct** student to provide examples of four text-structure types found in alternate text.	• **Provide** visual of Text-Structure Overview (T5) when student is answering questions; have student make test corrections; retest missed items. • **Use** guided interaction to discuss **Content Reader** Unit 4, and find text structure; have student make test corrections; retest missed items.

Points Scored for Part C

5 or fewer points = **Approaching Mastery**

6 points = **At Mastery**

5 or fewer points = **ELL**

Approaching Mastery	At Mastery	ELL
• **Have** student make check mark next to each step of decoding-multipart-words or context-clues strategies (T7) as each step is completed; have student make test corrections. • **Review** until firm decoding-multipart-words or context-clues strategies (T7) (see **Teacher's Edition** Units 1 and 2, Lessons 1–4, Part B); have student make test corrections.	• **Assign** student to "be the teacher," partnering with "approaching mastery" or ELL student to review decoding-multipart-words or context-clues strategies (T7). • **Assign** student to research one or more topics covered in **Content Reader** Unit 4; have student apply decoding-multipart-words or context-clues strategies (T7) to words in researched materials.	• **Use** primary language equivalents, cognates, pantomiming, or realia, when available, for targeted words; assist with test corrections; retest missed items. • **Provide** vowel chart as visual aid, and review vowel sounds; assist with test corrections; retest missed items.

Comprehension Strategies

Vocabulary Strategies

Unit 4 ✦ Assessment **97**

Skill or Strategy Taught	Units Recommended for General Education (Above Grade Level)	Units Recommended for General Education (At Grade Level)	Units Recommended for Reading Intervention and Special Education
	Lesson-Acceleration Chart		
Text connections	**1, 4** (Review as needed)	**1, 2, 4** (Review as needed)	Conduct all units
Decoding multipart words	**1, 4** (Review as needed)	**1, 2, 4** (Review as needed)	Conduct all units
Text structure	**2, 3, 7** (Review as needed)	**2–5, 7** (Review as needed)	Conduct all units
Context clues	**2, 5** (Review as needed)	**2, 3, 5** (Review as needed)	Conduct all units
Comprehension monitoring	**6, 8** (Review as needed)	**6–8** (Review as needed)	Conduct all units
Glossary use	**6, 9** (Review as needed)	**6, 7, 9** (Review as needed)	Conduct all units
Dictionary use	**7, 10** (Review as needed)	**7, 8, 10** (Review as needed)	Conduct all units
Online-dictionary use	**8, 11** (Review as needed)	**8, 9, 11** (Review as needed)	Conduct all units
SQ3R strategy	**8** (S) **9** (SQR) **10** (SQRR) **11** (SQ3R) **14, 15** (SQ3R) (Review as needed)	**8** (S) **9** (SQR) **10** (SQRR) **11** (SQ3R) **12–16** (SQ3R) (Review as needed)	Conduct all units
QHL strategy	**15, 18** (Review as needed)	**15, 16, 18** (Review as needed)	Conduct all units
Lecture note taking	**17, 20** (Review as needed)	**17, 18, 20** (Review as needed)	Conduct all units
Strategy Bookmark	**18, 20** (Review as needed)	**18–20** (Review as needed)	Conduct all units
Science and social studies textbook use	**21–25** (Review as needed)	**21–25** (Review as needed)	Conduct all units

Homework

Homework can be an important part of any adolescent literacy program and is meaningful only when students have acquired a skill. Students should not be provided homework on skills or strategies with strong or moderate teacher support; students should be independent in the use of the skill or strategy before you assign homework. If you choose to assign homework, you might consider the following ideas:

- "Beyond the Book" activities are provided whenever the program changes from content-area science text to social studies text or back again (after Units 2, 4, 8, 10, 14, 16, and 20). Because these activities center on program skills applied to many types of informational text (magazine articles, Web sites, maps, and so on), they could serve as a basis for homework. For example, a student could, as homework, make text connections using a newspaper article.

- The differentiated-instruction charts, at the end of every fifth lesson (beginning in Unit 2) in the Teacher's Edition, provide suggestions for students approaching mastery, students at mastery, and ELL students. These guidelines align with assessment performance but could be used as a basis from which to select homework activities. For example, each lesson in the Content Reader ends with an assessment activity that could be assigned as homework.

- In-class activities not fully completed during class may be sent home as homework. For example, during an SQ3R activity, students may not have time to apply the strategy to an entire section in the Content Reader or in their classroom science or social studies textbook; students could complete this at home.

- Whenever possible, students should take the skills and strategies they've learned and practice using them in their classroom science and social studies textbooks. You could coordinate efforts with content-area teachers to ensure students practice the learned skills and strategies on homework assigned by those teachers.

Sample Lessons

Unit 2, Lesson 1

By Unit 2, **Unit 1** activities have already been taught and include the following skills and strategies:

- Text connections
- Decoding-multipart-words strategy
- Oral and silent reading: fluency practice
- Think-pair-share strategy

Unit 2, Lesson 1, includes the following skills and strategies:

- Text connections
- Decoding-multipart-words strategy
- Oral reading: fluency practice (cold timing)

- Text structure
- Word-learning strategies (context clues)

Lesson 1 specifics across the **three instructional tracks** include the following:

Part A: Comprehension Strategies: Text Connections

- Using the Content Reader table of contents to find the assigned lesson.
- Working with partners to complete a text-connections chart in the Workbook.

Part A: Comprehension Strategies: Text Structure

- As a class, participating in activities introducing text structure and Description-or-List.

Part B: Vocabulary Strategies: Decoding-Multipart-Words Strategy

- Working with partners to complete a decoding-multipart-words strategy activity in the Workbook.

Part B: Vocabulary Strategies: Word-Learning Strategy: Context Clues

- As a class, participating in activities centered on word-learning strategies (context clues).

Part C: Fluency Strategies: Cold Timing

- Working with partners to complete a cold timing using the Unit 2 fluency passage.

Unit 2 • Lesson 1

Reading Skills and Strategies

- Make text connections.
- Identify text structure.
- Decode multipart words.
- Use word-learning strategies.

PART A | 20 minutes | TEACHER SUPPORT: STRONG | **MODERATE** | STUDENT INDEPENDENCE

Comprehension Strategies

Activity ▶ Text Connections

1.  **Direct** students to **Content Reader** page i.

2. On what page will you find Unit 2, Lesson 1? *18.* **Direct** students to page 18.

3. **Direct** students to **Workbook** page 13. **Show** Transparency 1: Text-Connections Chart (T1).

Transparency 1/Workbook page 13

ROUTINE • Making Text Connections

a. **Assign** student partners.

b. **Read** question 1 to students.
- What's the topic of the lesson?

c. **Ask** students to discuss question 1 and then to write the answer.

d. **Ask** students what they wrote. **Write** on T1. *Living Things*

e. **Repeat** steps b–d for question 2. *to learn more about living things*

f. **Repeat** steps b–d for question 3. **Accept** reasonable responses.

Content Reader

Unit 2
Science

Lesson 1 — **Living Things**

Reading Skills and Strategies
- Make text connections.
- Identify text structure.
- Decode multipart words.
- Use word-learning strategies.

As YOU Read!

What You'll Learn
- The characteristics of living things
- The needs of living things

Why It's Important
Cells are the basic unit of all living things.

Key Terms
- organisms
- cells
- stimulus
- autotrophs
- heterotrophs
- homeostasis

Living things, or **organisms,** can be as large as whales or so small you can't see them without a microscope. All the organisms on Earth are different. What do you think they have in common?

Characteristics of Living Things

All living things share six basic traits, or characteristics. First, living things are made of cells. Second, their cells contain chemicals that carry out various activities. Third, the cells of living things use energy to perform life functions. Fourth, all organisms respond to their environment. Fifth,

living things grow and develop. Sixth, all organisms reproduce.

Cellular Organization

Cells are the smallest parts of living things. They make up the form of an organism and carry out all the functions in the organism's body. Organisms may contain only one cell, or they may contain many cells. In multicelled organisms, cells are specially designed to do certain jobs. For example,

▶ A paramecium contains only one cell.

18 ⟩ Unit 2 ✦ Lesson 1

Activity ▶ | TEACHER SUPPORT: **STRONG** | MODERATE | STUDENT INDEPENDENCE

Text Structure

1. 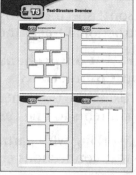 **Direct** students to **Content Reader** page 18.

2. Read Unit 2, Lesson 1, to yourself. **Allow** six minutes.

3. Textbook authors organize, or arrange, paragraphs in certain ways to help you gather meaning. This organizational arrangement is called text structure.

4. **Show** Transparency 5: Text-Structure Overview (T5).

5. **Point** to each type of text structure as you read each title.
- Description-or-List Chart
- Order-or-Sequence Chart
- Cause-and-Effect Chart
- Compare-and-Contrast Chart

6. **Ask** students to read aloud each text structure.

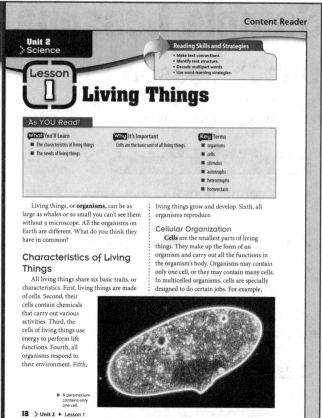

Transparency 5

Teacher's Edition: Unit 2, Lesson 1

▲ Human skin is made up of many cells.

center, direct all cell activity. Proteins and fats, or lipids, aid in cell growth and repair.

Energy

Starches, or carbohydrates, provide cells with energy. All the jobs cells do require energy to sustain life for the organism.

Response to Environment

Have you ever looked under a rock in the woods? You probably saw dozens of tiny bugs running in all directions. By lifting the rock, you shed light on their dark environment. The light was a **stimulus**, something that changed the bugs' surroundings and caused them to react. Their response was to run away from the light.

Growth and Development

Living things grow as they progress through their life cycle. They go through a series of changes that make them more complex. When living things are fully developed, they are able to reproduce, or produce offspring.

humans have skin cells, muscle cells, and blood cells that perform specific tasks within the body.

Chemicals

All cells contain chemicals necessary for life. Chemicals in the cell's nucleus, or control

▼ The drawing shows the life cycle of a frog.

Living Things **19**

7. Point to the Description-or-List Chart. Description-or-List is the most common way of organizing information in a textbook. That's why you'll learn about this type of text structure first. Description-or-List includes a main idea and supporting details.

8. What's a main idea? Idea: *The most important thing a paragraph is about.* **Accept** reasonable responses.

9. Where does a main idea usually appear in a paragraph? Idea: *In the first sentence in a paragraph.* **Accept** reasonable responses.

10. What are supporting details? Idea: *Statements that tell more about the main idea.* **Accept** reasonable responses.

11. Where do you usually find supporting details? Idea: *After the main idea.* **Accept** reasonable responses.

12. Direct students to **Content Reader** page 18: *Characteristics of Living Things,* paragraph 1. Read this paragraph to yourself. **Allow** one minute.

13. Show Transparency 6: Description-or-List Chart (T6).

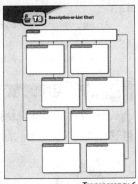

Transparency 6

ROUTINE · Using the Description-or-List Chart

a. I'll use the Description-or-List Chart for the **Content Reader** information I just read.

b. Model think-aloud for T6.

Think-Aloud Main Idea: First, I need to find the main idea of this paragraph, or the most important thing this paragraph is about. The main idea is usually the first sentence. **Read Content Reader** page 18: *Characteristics of Living Things,* paragraph 1, sentence 1. This sentence is the main idea because the meaning is general and it's also the first sentence. Six basic traits or characteristics should come next. I'll read to see if I'm right. **Read** the rest of paragraph 1. I'm right. The rest of the sentences give specific information about the first sentence. The first sentence is the main idea. I'll write *All living things share six basic traits or characteristics* in the box labeled "Main Idea."

Supporting Details: Next I need to find the supporting details about the main idea. Supporting details tell me more about the main idea. Supporting details usually follow the main idea. The main idea says there are six basic traits or characteristics. The rest of the sentences included these six basic traits or characteristics. **Read** the rest of paragraph 1 after sentence 1. I'll write one sentence in each "Supporting Detail" box. **Write** *Living things are made of cells. Their cells contain chemicals that carry out various activities. The cells of living things use energy to perform life functions. All organisms respond to their environment. Living things grow and develop. All organisms reproduce.* ❖

Unit 2 ✦ Lesson 1 **39**

Content Reader

14. When could you use the Description-or-List Chart?
Accept reasonable responses.

15. Why should you use the Description-or-List Chart?
Accept reasonable responses.

PART B | 15 minutes | TEACHER SUPPORT STRONG MODERATE STUDENT INDEPENDENCE

Vocabulary Strategies

Activity ▶ Decoding-Multipart-Words Strategy

1. [WB] 🖐 ⚫ **Direct** students to the first activity on **Workbook** page 14. **Show** Transparency 7: Context-Clues Strategy (T7).

Transparency 7/Workbook page 14

2. You've seen the top strategy before. It's the decoding-multipart-words strategy. The decoding-multipart-words strategy will now always appear on a page like this.

▲ By conducting an experiment, Redi discovered that flies and maggots do not spontaneously arise from meat.

Life Comes from Life

Long ago, people believed living things could come from nonliving things. This idea was disproved in 1668. At that time, people believed flies could spontaneously arise from meat. An Italian doctor named Francesco Redi conducted a controlled experiment. He covered one jar of meat. Another jar was left uncovered. Flies laid eggs on the uncovered meat. The eggs hatched into young flies called maggots. The covered meat showed no signs of maggots because flies could not enter the jar.

Even after Redi's experiment, many people still thought living things could arise from nonliving things. In the nineteenth century, a French chemist named Louis Pasteur set up some experiments. He showed that bacteria must already be present for new bacteria to appear. Pasteur's results convinced people that living things come only from other living things. This happens through reproduction.

20 ❯ Unit 2 ✦ Lesson 1

ROUTINE · Decoding Multipart Words

a. **Assign** student partners.

b. **Have** students write *organisms* in the "Word" box. **Write** on T7.

c. **Read** Step 1 to students.

• Step 1: Underline all the vowel sounds.

d. **Ask** students to discuss and complete Step 1.

e. **Ask** students what they did. **Write** on T7. **Review** vowel sounds as needed. *Organisms*.

f. **Read** Step 2 to students.

• Step 2: Make a slash between the word parts so each part has one vowel sound.

g. **Ask** students to discuss and complete Step 2.

h. **Ask** students what they did. **Write** on T7. **Review** vowel sounds as needed. Idea: *Or/gan/isms*.

i. **Read** Step 3 to students.

• Step 3: Go back to the beginning of the word, and read the parts in order.

j. **Ask** students to discuss and complete Step 3.

k. **Ask** students what they did. Idea: *Or/gan/isms*.

Teacher's Edition: Unit 2, Lesson 1

Content Reader

The Needs of Living Things

Despite the great diversity, or variety, of life, all living things must meet four basic needs to survive. Every organism must have food, water, a place to live, and stable conditions inside its body.

Food

Remember that organisms are made up of cells, and cells need energy. Living things must get energy from food in order to live. Some organisms, like green plants, can make their own food. They are called **autotrophs**. All other organisms are **heterotrophs**. Heterotrophs cannot make their own food. Heterotrophs must feed on other organisms for the energy they need. For example, a rabbit is a heterotroph. It eats a dandelion, an autotroph. A hawk is another heterotroph. It eats the rabbit.

Water

Water is important to life. Most organisms cannot live more than a few days without it. Living things need water to grow and to

reproduce. They need water to break down food and to get other chemicals from the environment.

A Place to Live

For an organism to survive, it must live in a place that meets its needs. Its surroundings must provide food, water, and adequate space. Autotrophs must get enough sunlight to make their own food.

Stable Internal Conditions

An organism's environment provides the resources for survival. However, its surroundings may change. An organism must be able to regulate the conditions inside its cells, even if the environment outside its body changes.

Homeostasis is the ability to maintain stable internal conditions within cells. Without homeostasis, living things could not adjust to changes in temperature, moisture, or chemicals in their environment. For example, desert animals conserve water in their bodies. The stored water helps them survive long periods without rain.

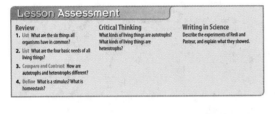

Lesson Assessment

Review
1. List What are the six things all organisms have in common?
2. List What are the four basic needs of all living things?
3. Compare and Contrast How are autotrophs and heterotrophs different?
4. Define What is a stimulus? What is homeostasis?

Critical Thinking
What kinds of living things are autotrophs? What kinds of living things are heterotrophs?

Writing in Science
Describe the experiments of Redi and Pasteur, and explain what they showed.

Living Things **21**

l. **Read** Step 4 to students.
• Step 4: Read the whole word.

m. **Ask** students to discuss and complete Step 4.

n. **Ask** students what they did. *Organisms.*

Activity | STRONG TEACHER SUPPORT — MODERATE — STUDENT INDEPENDENCE

Word-Learning Strategy: Context Clues

1. [CR] **Direct** students to **Content Reader** page 18.

2. Your textbooks often try to define new or difficult words. Sometimes the words are bold and highlighted. **Direct** students to **Content Reader** page 18: *Living Things*, paragraph 1, sentence 1, *organisms*. These words are bold and highlighted to draw your attention to them. Typically, the definitions of these bold and highlighted words come right before or right after the word.

3. What do you do when you're reading and come across a word you don't know? **Accept** reasonable responses.

4. 🌐 📖 **Show** T7. **Point** to the second activity. Now you'll learn a new strategy to help you figure out what words mean. It's called the context-clues strategy. Context clues are hints in the text that help you figure out the meanings of words. Sometimes these hints are obvious, such as bold and highlighted words. Sometimes these hints are not as obvious. You must continue reading the text to find out what the word means. Other times you must check another source because you can't find the word's meaning.

ROUTINE • Using the Context-Clues Strategy

a. **Read** steps 1–3 to students.
• Step 1: Read the sentence containing the word.
• Step 2: Look for a definition or for examples of the word in the sentence.
• Step 3: Read before or after the sentence for a definition or for examples of the word.

b. **Ask** students to read aloud steps 1–3.

c. **Direct** students to **Content Reader** page 18: *Living Things*, paragraph 1, sentence 1, *organisms*.

d. I'll use the context-clues strategy for the word *organisms*. I'll write my answer in the bottom box on this page. **Remind** students that *organisms* is a bold and highlighted word, so the hints may be obvious.

e. **Model** think-aloud for T7: Context-Clues Strategy.

Think-Aloud First, I'll read the sentence containing the word. **Read** sentence 1. Second, I'll look for a definition or for examples of the word in the sentence. Because *organisms* is a bold and highlighted word, the definition will be somewhere before or after the word. I see a definition right before the word, so I'll write *Living things* as the beginning of my definition. I'll write this under "Word Meaning from Context." **Read** the rest of paragraph 1 after sentence 1. I also see that a whale is an example of an organism, so I'll write *such as whales* as the end of my definition. The definition of the word *organisms* is *Living things, such as whales.* ❖

5. When could you use the context-clues strategy? **Accept** reasonable responses.

6. Why should you use the context-clues strategy? **Accept** reasonable responses.

Continued: Unit 2 ✦ Lesson 1 **41**

Teacher's Edition: Unit 2, Lesson 1

Continued: Unit 2 • Lesson 1

PART C — 10 minutes — STRONG — TEACHER SUPPORT MODERATE — STUDENT INDEPENDENCE

Fluency Strategies

Activity ▶ Cold Timing

> **NOTE:** The procedure for cold timing has been included below for teacher reference. As students become more familiar with the procedure, reduce teacher support to encourage student independence.

1. Remember, each week you'll do two timings with a partner. You'll do a cold timing at the beginning of the week and a hot timing at the end of the week to see how much you've improved.

2. 🧴🌐 **WB** **Direct** students to **Workbook** page 1 as needed. Show Transparency 3: Fluency Sample (T3) as needed.

Transparency 3/Workbook page 1

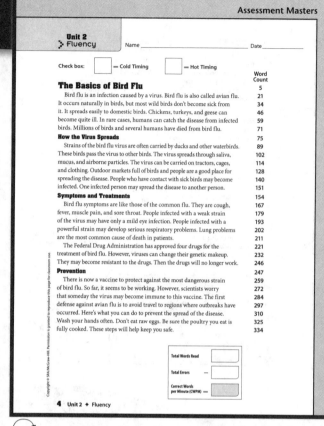

Unit 2
▶ Fluency

Name _____ Date _____

Check box: ☐ = Cold Timing ☐ = Hot Timing

	Word Count
The Basics of Bird Flu	5
Bird flu is an infection caused by a virus. Bird flu is also called avian flu.	21
It occurs naturally in birds, but most wild birds don't become sick from	34
it. It spreads easily to domestic birds. Chickens, turkeys, and geese can	46
become quite ill. In rare cases, humans can catch the disease from infected	59
birds. Millions of birds and several humans have died from bird flu.	71
How the Virus Spreads	75
Strains of the bird flu virus are often carried by ducks and other waterbirds.	89
These birds pass the virus to other birds. The virus spreads through saliva,	102
mucus, and airborne particles. The virus can be carried on tractors, cages,	114
and clothing. Outdoor markets full of birds and people are a good place for	128
spreading the disease. People who have contact with sick birds may become	140
infected. One infected person may spread the disease to another person.	151
Symptoms and Treatments	154
Bird flu symptoms are like those of the common flu. They are cough,	167
fever, muscle pain, and sore throat. People infected with a weak strain	179
of the virus may have only a mild eye infection. People infected with a	193
powerful strain may develop serious respiratory problems. Lung problems	202
are the most common cause of death in patients.	211
The Federal Drug Administration has approved four drugs for the	221
treatment of bird flu. However, viruses can change their genetic makeup.	232
They may become resistant to the drugs. Then the drugs will no longer work.	246
Prevention	247
There is now a vaccine to protect against the most dangerous strain	259
of bird flu. So far, it seems to be working. However, scientists worry	272
that someday the virus may become immune to this vaccine. The first	284
defense against avian flu is to avoid travel to regions where outbreaks have	297
occurred. Here's what you can do to prevent the spread of the disease.	310
Wash your hands often. Don't eat raw eggs. Be sure the poultry you eat is	325
fully cooked. These steps will help keep you safe.	334

Total Words Read ☐

Total Errors ☐

Correct Words per Minute (CWPM) = ☐

4 Unit 2 ✦ Fluency

3. **Review** the numbers on the right side of the sample passage, the procedures for conducting a timing, and the use of a slash at the end of the timing as needed.

4. Now you'll do your cold timing using a new fluency passage.

Teacher's Edition: Unit 2, Lesson 1

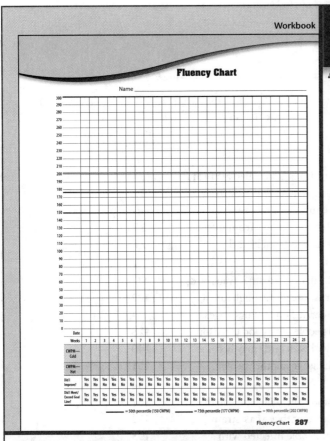

Workbook

Fluency Chart

Name _____

i. **Direct** students to **Workbook** page 287. **Review** Fluency Chart and goal-line procedures as needed. **Show** Transparency 4: Fluency Chart (T4).

j. **Have** students write their "CWPM—Cold" score on their Fluency Chart and graph their score in blue.

k. **Have** students check that what they wrote in the blue box matches what they graphed on their chart. **Have** students check their goal line.

5. All week you'll practice reading your fluency passage. At the end of the week, you'll do your hot timing to see how much you've improved. You'll also check to see whether you've reached your goal line.

Lesson Wrap-Up

Conclude lesson with a brief review of reading skills and strategies taught (make text connections, identify text structure, decode multipart words, and use word-learning strategies).

ROUTINE · Conducting Cold Timing

a. **Assign** student partners. **Reproduce** Unit 2 Fluency, **Assessment Masters** page 4. **Provide** blue pens.

b. **Ask** Partner 1 to read aloud to Partner 2. **Remind** students not to interrupt.

c. **Time** students for one minute. **Monitor** students.

d. **Ask** Partner 2 to tell Partner 1 each word missed, and ask Partner 1 to read aloud each sentence correctly. **Review** how to correct an error as needed.

e. **Ask** Partner 2 to read aloud to Partner 1. **Remind** students not to interrupt.

f. **Time** students for one minute. **Monitor** students.

g. **Ask** Partner 1 to tell Partner 2 each word missed, and ask Partner 2 to read aloud each sentence correctly. **Review** how to correct an error as needed.

h. **Have** students calculate CWPM. **Guide** as needed. **Provide** students with calculators as needed.

Continued: Unit 2 ✦ Lesson 1 **43**

Teacher's Edition: Unit 2, Lesson 1

Unit 2
⠿ Fluency

Name _____ Date _____

Check box: ☐ = Cold Timing   ☐ = Hot Timing

	Word Count
The Basics of Bird Flu	5
Bird flu is an infection caused by a virus. Bird flu is also called avian flu.	21
It occurs naturally in birds, but most wild birds don't become sick from	34
it. It spreads easily to domestic birds. Chickens, turkeys, and geese can	46
become quite ill. In rare cases, humans can catch the disease from infected	59
birds. Millions of birds and several humans have died from bird flu.	71
How the Virus Spreads	75
Strains of the bird flu virus are often carried by ducks and other waterbirds.	89
These birds pass the virus to other birds. The virus spreads through saliva,	102
mucus, and airborne particles. The virus can be carried on tractors, cages,	114
and clothing. Outdoor markets full of birds and people are a good place for	128
spreading the disease. People who have contact with sick birds may become	140
infected. One infected person may spread the disease to another person.	151
Symptoms and Treatments	154
Bird flu symptoms are like those of the common flu. They are cough,	167
fever, muscle pain, and sore throat. People infected with a weak strain	179
of the virus may have only a mild eye infection. People infected with a	193
powerful strain may develop serious respiratory problems. Lung problems	202
are the most common cause of death in patients.	211
The Federal Drug Administration has approved four drugs for the	221
treatment of bird flu. However, viruses can change their genetic makeup.	232
They may become resistant to the drugs. Then the drugs will no longer work.	246
Prevention	247
There is now a vaccine to protect against the most dangerous strain	259
of bird flu. So far, it seems to be working. However, scientists worry	272
that someday the virus may become immune to this vaccine. The first	284
defense against avian flu is to avoid travel to regions where outbreaks have	297
occurred. Here's what you can do to prevent the spread of the disease.	310
Wash your hands often. Don't eat raw eggs. Be sure the poultry you eat is	325
fully cooked. These steps will help keep you safe.	334

Total Words Read ☐

Total Errors − ☐

Correct Words per Minute (CWPM) = ☐

4 Unit 2 ✦ Fluency

 **Text-Connections Chart**

1

What's the topic of the lesson? _____

_____

_____

2

What's your purpose for reading? _____

_____

_____

3

What do you know about the topic? _____

_____

_____

_____

_____

_____

_____

_____

_____

_____

Fluency Sample

Check box: ☐ = Cold Timing   ☐ = Hot Timing

Word Count

Dian Fossey

	Word Count
Dian Fossey	2
Dian Fossey was a famous scientist who studied mountain gorillas.	12
She had been interested in animals her whole life. She went to college as a	27
preveterinary student. But then Fossey changed her major to occupational	37
therapy so she could help people learn to live and work independently.	49
Fossey worked for many years as an occupational therapist.	58
Fossey became interested in gorillas after she read a book about them by	71
a zoologist. A zoologist is a scientist who studies animals. Fossey traveled	83
to Africa and spent six weeks there. While in Africa, she met Dr. Louis	97
Leakey, a famous scientist, who later asked her to return to Africa to study	111
gorillas. Fossey agreed. Her life would forever be changed.	120
Fossey lived among the gorillas for almost eighteen years. She spent	131
countless hours watching the gorillas, living among them, and imitating	141
their behaviors and sounds so she could earn their trust. Fossey was	153
so interested in gorillas she studied about them intensely, earning her	164
doctorate from Cambridge University in 1976. She later became a professor	175
at Cornell University and wrote a book about her experiences, *Gorillas in*	187
the Mist. This book is one of the best-selling books about gorillas of all	201
time. In fact, the book was so popular it became a movie.	213
One day, when a gorilla touched Fossey's hand, she became the first	225
known person ever to have voluntary contact with a gorilla. She became	237
very close to one gorilla. She named this gorilla Digit. Fossey watched	249
Digit grow, and the two of them became very close. Digit was later killed	263
by poachers. Poachers are people who kill animals that are endangered	274
or that live on protected land. Fossey was so upset over Digit's death she	288
developed the Digit Fund (now called the Dian Fossey Gorilla Fund) to	300
raise money for the protection of gorillas.	307
In 1985, Fossey was killed. Her death is still considered an unsolved	319
mystery. Her dream was to preserve the safety of gorillas and to watch	332
their numbers grow.	335

Total Words Read	☐
Total Errors	— ☐
Correct Words per Minute (CWPM)	= ☐

Fluency Chart

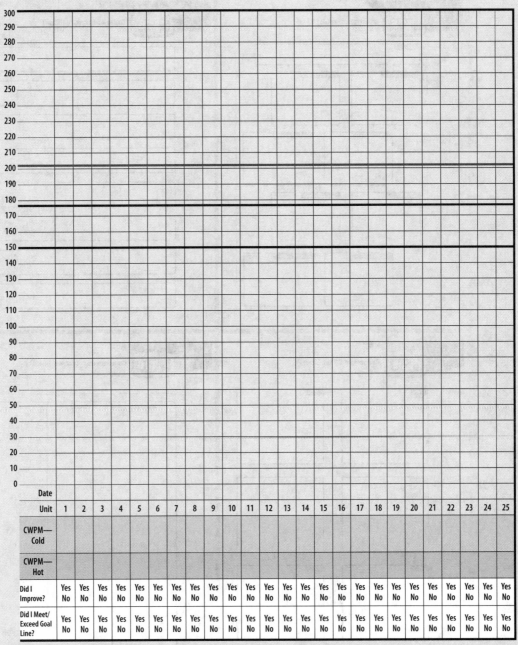

| | = 50th percentile (150 CWPM) | | = 75th percentile (177 CWPM) | | = 90th percentile (202 CWPM) |

T5 Text-Structure Overview

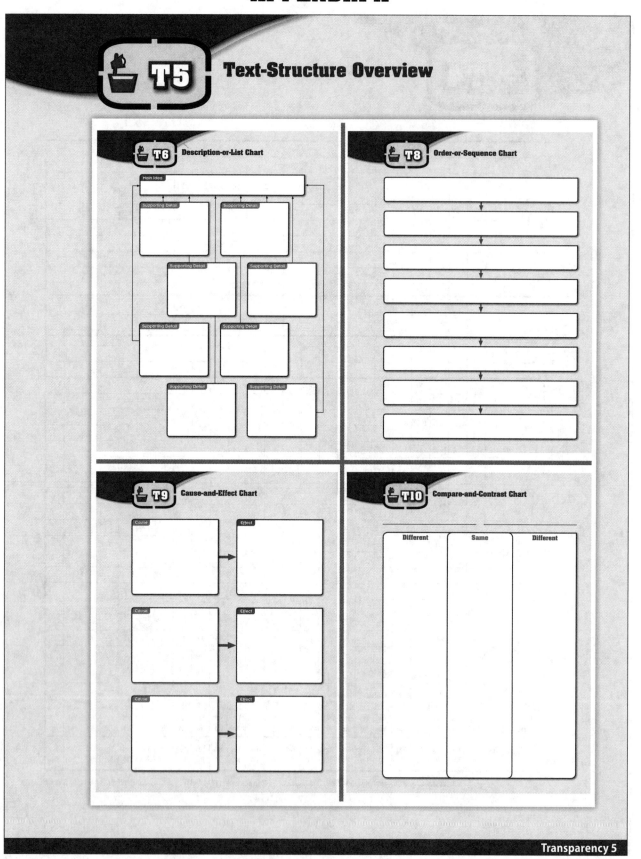

T6 Description-or-List Chart

Main Idea

Supporting Detail

Supporting Detail

Supporting Detail

Supporting Detail

Supporting Detail

Supporting Detail

Supporting Detail

Supporting Detail

T8 Order-or-Sequence Chart

T9 Cause-and-Effect Chart

Cause — Effect

Cause — Effect

Cause — Effect

T10 Compare-and-Contrast Chart

Different	Same	Different

Transparency 5

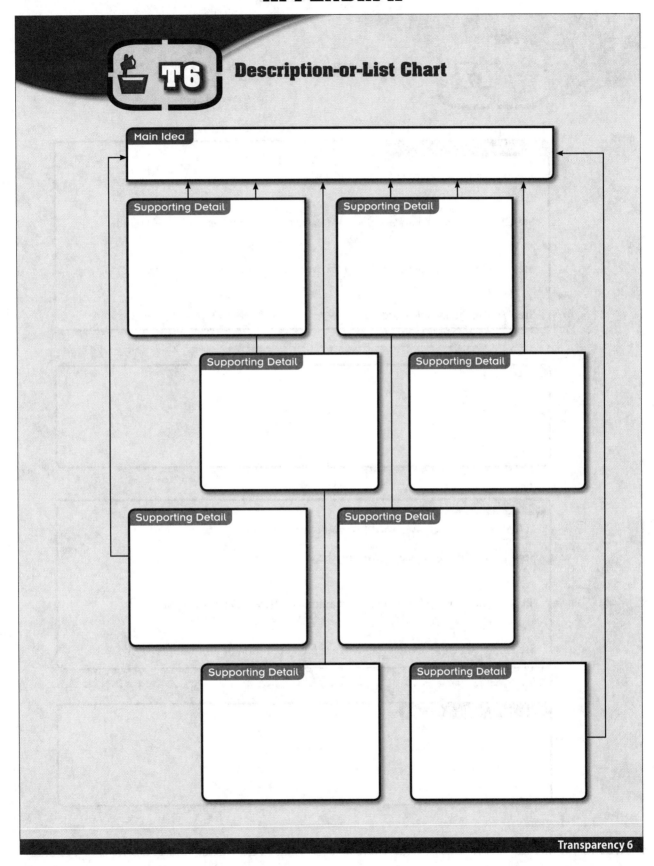

T6 — Description-or-List Chart

Main Idea

Supporting Detail

Supporting Detail

Supporting Detail

Supporting Detail

Supporting Detail

Supporting Detail

Supporting Detail

Supporting Detail

Transparency 6

 **Context-Clues Strategy**

Decoding-Multipart-Words Strategy

Step 1: Underline all the vowel sounds.

Step 2: Make a slash between the word parts so each part has one vowel sound.

Step 3: Go back to the beginning of the word, and read the parts in order.

Step 4: Read the whole word.

Word

Context-Clues Strategy

When you come across a word you don't know,

Step 1: Read the sentence containing the word.

Step 2: Look for a definition or for examples of the word in the sentence.

Step 3: Read before or after the sentence for a definition or for examples of the word.

Word Meaning from Context

Transparency 7

Unit 2 :> Science

Lesson 1

Living Things

Reading Skills and Strategies
- Make text connections.
- Identify text structure.
- Decode multipart words.
- Use word-learning strategies.

As YOU Read!

What You'll Learn
- The characteristics of living things
- The needs of living things

Why It's Important
Cells are the basic unit of all living things.

Key Terms
- organisms
- cells
- stimulus
- autotrophs
- heterotrophs
- homeostasis

Living things, or **organisms,** can be as large as whales or so small you can't see them without a microscope. All the organisms on Earth are different. What do you think they have in common?

Characteristics of Living Things

All living things share six basic traits, or characteristics. First, living things are made of cells. Second, their cells contain chemicals that carry out various activities. Third, the cells of living things use energy to perform life functions. Fourth, all organisms respond to their environment. Fifth,

living things grow and develop. Sixth, all organisms reproduce.

Cellular Organization

Cells are the smallest parts of living things. They make up the form of an organism and carry out all the functions in the organism's body. Organisms may contain only one cell, or they may contain many cells. In multicelled organisms, cells are specially designed to do certain jobs. For example,

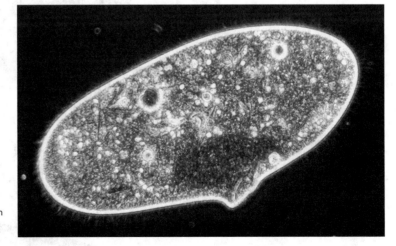

▶ A paramecium contains only one cell.

18 :> Unit 2 ♦ Lesson 1

Content Reader: Unit 2, Lesson 1

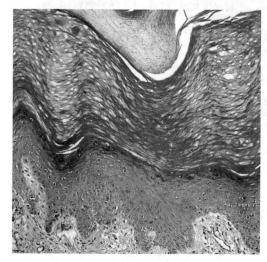

▲ Human skin is made up of many cells.

humans have skin cells, muscle cells, and blood cells that perform specific tasks within the body.

Chemicals

All cells contain chemicals necessary for life. Chemicals in the cell's nucleus, or control center, direct all cell activity. Proteins and fats, or lipids, aid in cell growth and repair.

Energy

Starches, or carbohydrates, provide cells with energy. All the jobs cells do require energy to sustain life for the organism.

Response to Environment

Have you ever looked under a rock in the woods? You probably saw dozens of tiny bugs running in all directions. By lifting the rock, you shed light on their dark environment. The light was a **stimulus,** something that changed the bugs' surroundings and caused them to react. Their response was to run away from the light.

Growth and Development

Living things grow as they progress through their life cycle. They go through a series of changes that make them more complex. When living things are fully developed, they are able to reproduce, or produce offspring.

▼ The drawing shows the life cycle of a frog.

Living Things 19

▲ By conducting an experiment, Redi discovered that flies and maggots do not spontaneously arise from meat.

Life Comes from Life

Long ago, people believed living things could come from nonliving things. This idea was disproved in 1668. At that time, people believed flies could spontaneously arise from meat. An Italian doctor named Francesco Redi conducted a controlled experiment. He covered one jar of meat. Another jar was left uncovered. Flies laid eggs on the uncovered meat. The eggs hatched into young flies called maggots. The covered meat showed no signs of maggots because flies could not enter the jar.

Even after Redi's experiment, many people still thought living things could arise from nonliving things. In the nineteenth century, a French chemist named Louis Pasteur set up some experiments. He showed that bacteria must already be present for new bacteria to appear. Pasteur's results convinced people that living things come only from other living things. This happens through reproduction.

20 ⯈ **Unit 2 ◆ Lesson 1**

The Needs of Living Things

Despite the great diversity, or variety, of life, all living things must meet four basic needs to survive. Every organism must have food, water, a place to live, and stable conditions inside its body.

Food

Remember that organisms are made up of cells, and cells need energy. Living things must get energy from food in order to live. Some organisms, like green plants, can make their own food. They are called **autotrophs.** All other organisms are **heterotrophs.** Heterotrophs cannot make their own food. Heterotrophs must feed on other organisms for the energy they need. For example, a rabbit is a heterotroph. It eats a dandelion, an autotroph. A hawk is another heterotroph. It eats the rabbit.

Water

Water is important to life. Most organisms cannot live more than a few days without it. Living things need water to grow and to reproduce. They need water to break down food and to get other chemicals from the environment.

A Place to Live

For an organism to survive, it must live in a place that meets its needs. Its surroundings must provide food, water, and adequate space. Autotrophs must get enough sunlight to make their own food.

Stable Internal Conditions

An organism's environment provides the resources for survival. However, its surroundings may change. An organism must be able to regulate the conditions inside its cells, even if the environment outside its body changes.

Homeostasis is the ability to maintain stable internal conditions within cells. Without homeostasis, living things could not adjust to changes in temperature, moisture, or chemicals in their environment. For example, desert animals conserve water in their bodies. The stored water helps them survive long periods without rain.

Lesson Assessment

Review

1. **List** What are the six things all organisms have in common?

2. **List** What are the four basic needs of all living things?

3. **Compare and Contrast** How are autotrophs and heterotrophs different?

4. **Define** What is a stimulus? What is homeostasis?

Critical Thinking

What kinds of living things are autotrophs? What kinds of living things are heterotrophs?

Writing in Science

Describe the experiments of Redi and Pasteur, and explain what they showed.

Unit 2
Science

Activity 1

Lesson 1

Text-Connections Chart

Name _____ Date _____

1

What's the topic of the lesson? _____

_____

_____

2

What's your purpose for reading? _____

_____

_____

3

What do you know about the topic? _____

_____

_____

_____

_____

_____

_____

_____

_____

_____

Unit 2 ✦ Lesson 1 ✦ Activity 1 Text-Connections Chart **13**

Unit 2
Science

Activity 2

Lesson 1

Context-Clues Strategy

Name _____ Date _____

Decoding-Multipart-Words Strategy

Step 1: Underline all the vowel sounds.

Step 2: Make a slash between the word parts so each part has one vowel sound.

Step 3: Go back to the beginning of the word, and read the parts in order.

Step 4: Read the whole word.

Word

Context-Clues Strategy

When you come across a word you don't know,

Step 1: Read the sentence containing the word.

Step 2: Look for a definition or for examples of the word in the sentence.

Step 3: Read before or after the sentence for a definition or for examples of the word.

Word Meaning from Context

14 Unit 2 ✦ Lesson 1 ✦ Activity 2 Context-Clues Strategy

Unit 9, Lesson 2

By Unit 9, **Units 1–8** activities have already been taught and include the following skills and strategies:

- Text structure
- Comprehension monitoring
- Decoding-multipart-words strategy
- Word-learning strategies (context clues, glossary)
- Oral and silent reading: fluency practice
- Think-pair-share strategy

- Word-learning strategies (dictionary)

- SQ3R strategy ("Survey," with integrated text connections)
- Word-learning strategies (online dictionary)

Unit 9, Lesson 2, includes the following skills and strategies:

- Text structure
- Comprehension monitoring
- Decoding-multipart-words strategy
- Word-learning strategies (context clues, glossary, dictionary)
- Oral and silent reading: fluency practice
- Think-pair-share strategy

- SQ3R strategy ("Survey," with integrated text connections)
- Word-learning strategies (online dictionary)

- SQ3R strategy ("Question," "Read")

Lesson 2 specifics across the **three instructional tracks** include the following:

Part A: Comprehension Strategies: SQ3R Strategy: Survey

- Using the Content Reader table of contents to find the assigned lesson.
- Working with partners to complete SQ3R-strategy "Survey" steps and use the SQ3R-Strategy Checklist in the Workbook.

Part A: Comprehension Strategies: SQ3R Strategy: Question, Read

- As a class, participating in activities centered on SQ3R-strategy "Question" and "Read" steps.

Part B: Vocabulary Strategies: Word-Learning Strategy: Context Clues

- Working with partners to complete a context-clues-strategy activity in the Workbook.

Part B: Vocabulary Strategies: Word-Learning Strategy: Glossary Use

- Working with partners to complete a glossary activity in the Workbook.

Part B: Vocabulary Strategies: Word-Learning Strategy: Dictionary Use

- Working with partners to complete a dictionary activity in the Workbook.

Part B: Vocabulary Strategies: Word-Learning Strategy: Online-Dictionary Use

- Working with partners to complete an online-dictionary activity in the Workbook.

Part C: Fluency Strategies: Decoding-Multipart-Words Strategy

- Working with partners to read the Unit 9 fluency passage silently and complete a decoding-multipart-words strategy activity in the Workbook.

Unit 9 · Lesson 2

Reading Skills and Strategies

- Use the SQ3R strategy.
- Use an online dictionary.

PART A ⏱ 25 minutes | STRONG | **TEACHER SUPPORT** MODERATE | STUDENT INDEPENDENCE

Comprehension Strategies

Activity ▸ SQ3R Strategy: Survey

1. 📖 **Direct** students to **Content Reader** page iii.

2. Turn to Unit 9, Lesson 2. What page did you turn to? *112.*

3. 📓🎓💿 **Direct** students to **Workbook** page 116. **Show** Transparency 12: SQ3R-Strategy Checklist (T12).

Transparency 12/ Workbook page 116

ROUTINE • Using the SQ3R Strategy: Survey

a. **Assign** student partners.

b. **Have** students make text connections on their own and then discuss with their partners what connections they made. **Monitor** students. **Guide** as needed.

c. **Ask** students what text connections they made.
Question 1: *The Panama Canal*
Question 2: *to learn more about the Panama Canal*
Question 3: **Accept** reasonable responses.

d. **Have** students make a check mark in the "Yes" box next to Step 1.

e. **Ask** students to read aloud "Survey" Step 2.

f. **Ask** students to discuss and to complete Step 2 and then to make a check mark in the "Yes" box next to Step 2.

g. **Ask** students what they surveyed in the beginning of the lesson. **Accept** reasonable responses. **Make** a check mark in the "Yes" box next to Step 2.

h. **Repeat** steps e–g for "Survey" steps 3 and 4.

Content Reader

Unit 9
▸ Social Studies

Reading Skills and Strategies
- Use the SQ3R strategy.
- Use an online dictionary.

Lesson 2 The Panama Canal

As YOU Read!

What You'll Learn
■ Why building the Panama Canal posed challenges
■ How the United States obtained control of the Panama Canal

Why It's Important
The story of the Panama Canal shows how economic and military considerations affect government decisions.

Key Terms
■ canal
■ lock

Everyone likes shortcuts. They save time and effort. As early as 1850, shipping companies and American presidents were pushing for a shortcut between the Atlantic and the Pacific Oceans.

Early Efforts

For years, any ship sailing from New York to San Francisco had to go around the tip of South America—a voyage of thirteen thousand miles. A **canal**, or artificial waterway, through Central America would eliminate 60 percent of the distance. The best locations for a canal were Nicaragua and Panama.

Every American president since Ulysses S. Grant considered building a canal through Central America. A canal would save businesses time and money, and it would help the military. Battleships had no quick route between the Atlantic and the Pacific. The navy would face critical delays if the United States ever fought a war on both oceans. However, the French, not the Americans, were the first to try building a canal.

Since 1821, Panama had been part of Colombia. In 1881, Colombia sold land in Panama to a French company for a canal. Once the work began, the builders faced many challenges. A mountain range stood in the way, and mud slides erased much of the workers' progress. Worst of all, tropical diseases, such as malaria and yellow fever, killed twenty-five thousand workers. After a few years, the company ran out of money, and the canal was left unfinished.

The United States Steps In

In early 1902, President Theodore Roosevelt asked the House of Representatives for $140 million to build a canal across Nicaragua. Instead, Congress approved funds to buy the land from the French company and complete the route through Panama. Roosevelt offered $10 million and an annual rent of $250,000 to Colombian officials for the right to build the canal. Colombia refused the offer.

112 ▸ Unit 9 ◆ Lesson 2

Activity ▸ | STRONG | **TEACHER SUPPORT** MODERATE | STUDENT INDEPENDENCE

SQ3R Strategy: Question, Read

1. 📓🎓💿 **Direct** students to **Workbook** page 117. **Show** Transparency 13: Note-Taking Form (T13).

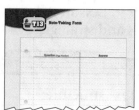

Transparency 13/Workbook page 117

2. As you know, you can use the Note-Taking Form to take notes from lessons in your **Content Reader.** You can also use the SQ3R-Strategy Checklist to complete the Q for "Question" and the first R for "Read."

ROUTINE • Using the SQ3R Strategy: Question, Read

a. 🎓💿 **Show** T12. **Read** "Question" and "Read" instructions to students.

- **Question:** One section at a time, change the lesson title, subheads, or bold and highlighted words into *who, what, where, when, why,* or *how* questions.

---

190 Unit 9 ✦ Lesson 2

Content Reader

Roosevelt decided to support a rebellion in Panama. A rebellion is a violent action by a large group of people to change a country's government.

◀ Many Americans criticized Roosevelt's interference in Latin American affairs.

An agent of the French canal company gathered a small army of Panamanians. On November 3, 1903, this group took over Panama City and declared independence from Colombia. Two days later, an American warship reached the coast of Panama and sent four hundred marines ashore. Eight more American warships formed a blockade to keep out Colombian ships. Roosevelt recognized the rebels as the new leaders of Panama, and the rebels gave the United States the right to build and control a canal.

Overcoming Difficulties

Building the canal might have been impossible if tropical diseases had gone unchecked. Fortunately, doctors had recently discovered that mosquitoes spread malaria and yellow fever. Mosquitoes need swamps or other standing water to multiply. The canal company hired a crew to fill swamps, cover water containers, and kill mosquitoes. Even so, of the 5,609 people who died while building the canal, many were victims of disease.

About 45,000 workers, most of them from the Caribbean, dug the canal. In addition to digging, they built locks and a dam. The **locks** adjusted water levels to raise and lower ships. Locks were necessary because the canal went through mountains. A dam was necessary to construct a lake for ships to sail across to the other side of Panama. The canal took eight years to complete. The dream of a passageway between oceans was realized.

◀ The canal is roughly fifty miles long. A ship can cross it in about eight hours.

Lesson Assessment

Review

1. **Explain** How would a canal help businesses and the military?

2. **Describe** How do locks help ships cross the Panama Canal?

3. **Summarize** What challenges did canal builders face?

4. **Conclude** Why did more workers die of tropical diseases during the canal project in the 1880s than during the project in the early twentieth century?

5. **Judge** Do you approve or disapprove of Roosevelt's support for the rebellion in Panama? Give reasons for your answer.

Critical Thinking
Why, do you think, did the French canal company organize the rebellion in Panama?

Writing in Social Studies
Write lyrics for a song about the Panama Canal to the tune of one of your favorite songs.

The Panama Canal   113

- **Read:** One section at a time, read any question, and write the answer. Reread, and adjust reading rate as needed.

b. **Call** on students to read aloud "Question" and "Read" instructions.

c. **Direct** students to **Content Reader** page 112: *The Panama Canal*, paragraph 1; *Early Efforts*, paragraphs 1–3.

d. **Show** T13. **Have** students copy everything you write as you model think-aloud for T13.

Think-Aloud Now that I've surveyed my lesson, I need to change the title, subheads, and bold and highlighted words into *who, what, when, where, why,* or *how* questions one section at a time. Then I'll read to answer the questions. Sometimes, after reading the section, I might need to change my questions to better fit the text. **Point** at **Content Reader** page 112: *The Panama Canal.* The lesson title is *The Panama Canal,* so my first question is *What is the Panama Canal? (page 112)* I'll write this in the column labeled "Question (Page Number)." Now I need to read the **Content Reader** and answer this first question. I also

need to think about whether my question makes sense. There is only one paragraph to read in this section. If I don't understand what I'm reading, I should reread it and adjust my reading rate. **Read** aloud paragraph 1. When I answer my question, I need to summarize, or write a brief description of the most important information I learned. My first question makes sense, so my first answer is *A shortcut for ships between the Atlantic and Pacific oceans.* I'll write this in the column labeled "Answer."

Point at **Content Reader** page 112: *Early Efforts.* The first subhead is *Early Efforts,* so my second question is *What were the early efforts? (page 112)* I'll write this in the column labeled "Question (Page Number)." Now I need to read the **Content Reader** and answer this question. I also need to think about whether my question makes sense. There are three paragraphs to read in this section. If I don't understand what I'm reading, I need to reread and adjust my reading rate. **Read** aloud paragraphs 1–3. My second question makes sense, so I'll summarize what I read to answer the question. My answer is *Because ships had to travel thirteen thousand miles around South America to get from New York to San Francisco, U.S. considered building canal through Central America. In 1881 France bought land from Colombia to build canal but failed.* I'll write this in the column labeled "Answer" across from my second question—*What were the early efforts?* This summary answers the question and includes details from each of the three paragraphs.

Point at **Content Reader** page 112: *Early Efforts,* paragraph 1, sentence 2, *canal.* The first bold and highlighted word is *canal.* I'll write a third question—*What is a canal? (page 112).* Now I need to read the **Content Reader** and answer this question. I also need to think about whether my question makes sense. I'll use the context-clues strategy to find the definition of the word. **Read** **Content Reader** page 112: *Early Efforts,* paragraph 1, sentences 2, 1, and 3. My third question makes sense based on what I read. My third answer is *An artificial waterway.* I'll write this in the column labeled "Answer" across from my third question—*What is a canal?*

Continue writing and answering questions for any subheads and bold and highlighted words in **Content Reader** Lesson 2 as time permits. ❖

Teacher's Edition: Unit 9, Lesson 2

e. **Show** T12 as you model think-aloud for T12.

(Think-Aloud) Now that I've written questions and have read the **Content Reader** to answer the questions, I need to use the SQ3R-Strategy Checklist. I'll make check marks in the "Yes" boxes next to "Question" and "Read." **Make** check marks in the "Yes" boxes next to "Question" and "Read." ❖

3. When could you use the Note-Taking Form? Why should you use the Note-Taking Form? **Accept** reasonable responses.

4. When could you question and read your lesson? Why should you question and read your lesson? **Accept** reasonable responses.

PART B ⏱ 10 minutes | **TEACHER SUPPORT** STRONG — MODERATE — STUDENT INDEPENDENCE

Vocabulary Strategies

Activity ▶ Word-Learning Strategy: Context Clues

> **NOTE:** If students did not read **Content Reader** Lesson 2 in its entirety in Part A, allow three minutes for students to read Lesson 2 before you continue.

1. [WB] 📚 🌐 **Direct** students to the first activity on **Workbook** page 118. **Show** Transparency 11: Word-Learning Strategies (T11) as needed.

Transparency 11/Workbook page 118

ROUTINE · Using the Context-Clues Strategy

a. **Assign** student partners.

b. [CR] **Direct** students to **Content Reader** page 112: *The United States Steps In*, paragraph 1, sentence 5.

c. **Have** students write *rebellion* next to "Word." **Write** on T11 as needed.

d. **Have** students use on their own the context-clues strategy and then discuss with their partners what they did. **Monitor** students. **Guide** as needed.

e. **Ask** students what they did. **Write** on T11 as needed. Idea: *A violent action by a large group of people to change a country's government*

Unit 9
Social Studies

Reading Skills and Strategies
- Use the SQ3R strategy.
- Use an online dictionary.

Lesson 2 The Panama Canal

As YOU Read!

What You'll Learn
- Why building the Panama Canal posed challenges
- How the United States obtained control of the Panama Canal

Why It's Important
The story of the Panama Canal shows how economic and military considerations affect government decisions.

Key Terms
- canal
- lock

Everyone likes shortcuts. They save time and effort. As early as 1850, shipping companies and American presidents were pushing for a shortcut between the Atlantic and the Pacific Oceans.

Early Efforts

For years, any ship sailing from New York to San Francisco had to go around the tip of South America—a voyage of thirteen thousand miles. A **canal**, or artificial waterway, through Central America would eliminate 60 percent of the distance. The best locations for a canal were Nicaragua and Panama.

Every American president since Ulysses S. Grant considered building a canal through Central America. A canal would save businesses time and money, and it would help the military. Battleships had no quick route between the Atlantic and the Pacific. The navy would face critical delays if the United States ever fought a war on both oceans. However, the French, not the Americans, were the first to try building a canal.

Since 1821, Panama had been part of Colombia. In 1881, Colombia sold land in Panama to a French company for a canal. Once the work began, the builders faced many challenges. A mountain range stood in the way, and mud slides erased much of the workers' progress. Worst of all, tropical diseases, such as malaria and yellow fever, killed twenty-five thousand workers. After a few years, the company ran out of money, and the canal was left unfinished.

The United States Steps In

In early 1902, President Theodore Roosevelt asked the House of Representatives for $140 million to build a canal across Nicaragua. Instead, Congress approved funds to buy the land from the French company and complete the route through Panama. Roosevelt offered $10 million and an annual rent of $250,000 to Colombian officials for the right to build the canal. Colombia refused the offer.

112 ⟩ Unit 9 ✦ Lesson 2

Activity ▶ | **TEACHER SUPPORT** STRONG — MODERATE — STUDENT INDEPENDENCE

Word-Learning Strategy: Glossary Use

1. [CR] **Direct** students to **Content Reader** page 260.

2. [WB] 📚 🌐 **Direct** students to the second activity on **Workbook** page 118. **Show** T11 as needed.

ROUTINE · Using a Glossary

a. **Assign** student partners.

b. **Have** students find and write on their own the glossary definition of *rebellion* and then discuss with their partners what they wrote. **Monitor** students. **Guide** as needed.

c. **Ask** students what they wrote. **Write** on T11 as needed. *A violent action by a large group of people to change a country's government*

Content Reader

Roosevelt decided to support a rebellion in Panama. A rebellion is a violent action by a large group of people to change a country's government.

◄ Many Americans criticized Roosevelt's interference in Latin American affairs.

An agent of the French canal company gathered a small army of Panamanians. On November 3, 1903, this group took over Panama City and declared independence from Colombia. Two days later, an American warship reached the coast of Panama and sent four hundred marines ashore. Eight more American warships formed a blockade to keep out Colombian ships. Roosevelt recognized the rebels as the new leaders of Panama, and the rebels gave the United States the right to build and control a canal.

Overcoming Difficulties

Building the canal might have been impossible if tropical diseases had gone unchecked. Fortunately, doctors had recently discovered that mosquitoes spread malaria and yellow fever. Mosquitoes need swamps or other standing water to multiply. The canal company hired a crew to fill swamps, cover water containers, and kill mosquitoes. Even so, of the 5,609 people who died while building the canal, many were victims of disease.

About 45,000 workers, most of them from the Caribbean, dug the canal. In addition to digging, they built locks and a dam. The **locks** adjusted water levels to raise and lower ships. Locks were necessary because the canal went through mountains. A dam was necessary to construct a lake for ships to sail across to the other side of Panama. The canal took eight years to complete. The dream of a passageway between oceans was realized.

◄ The canal is roughly fifty miles long. A ship can cross it in about eight hours.

Lesson Assessment

Review

1. **Explain** How would a canal help businesses and the military?

2. **Describe** How do locks help ships cross the Panama Canal?

3. **Summarize** What challenges did canal builders face?

4. **Conclude** Why did more workers die of tropical diseases during the canal project in the 1880s than during the project in the early twentieth century?

5. **Judge** Do you approve or disapprove of Roosevelt's support for the rebellion in Panama? Give reasons for your answer.

Critical Thinking

Why, do you think, did the French canal company organize the rebellion in Panama?

Writing in Social Studies

Write lyrics for a song about the Panama Canal to the tune of one of your favorite songs.

The Panama Canal **113**

Activity ▶
STRONG · MODERATE · STUDENT INDEPENDENCE

Word-Learning Strategy: Dictionary Use

1. 🔲 🧰 ⬤ **Provide** dictionaries to students. **Direct** students to the third activity on **Workbook** page 118. **Show** T11.

ROUTINE · Using a Dictionary

a. **Assign** student partners.

b. **Have** students find *rebellion* and its dictionary definition.

c. **Ask** students to discuss and then to write the definition in the "Dictionary Definition" box. **Monitor** students. **Guide** as needed.

d. **Ask** students what they wrote. **Write** on T11.

Activity ▶
STRONG · MODERATE · STUDENT INDEPENDENCE

Word-Learning Strategy: Online-Dictionary Use

> **NOTE:** If unable to provide a computer to each student, provide to small groups, or use electronic spell-checkers.

---

1. 🔲 🧰 ⬤ **Provide** students with access to an online dictionary. **Direct** students to the last activity on **Workbook** page 118. **Show** T11.

ROUTINE · Using an Online Dictionary

a. **Assign** student partners.

b. **Ask** how to find the definition of *rebellion* with an online dictionary. **Accept** reasonable responses.

c. **Have** students find *rebellion* and its online-dictionary definition.

d. **Ask** students to discuss and then to write the definition in the "Online-Dictionary Definition" box.

e. **Ask** students what they wrote. **Write** on T11.

f. **Discuss** glossary, dictionary, and online-dictionary definitions with students.

PART **C** ⏱ 10 minutes · STRONG · MODERATE · STUDENT INDEPENDENCE · TEACHER SUPPORT

Fluency Strategies

Activity Decoding-Multipart-Words Strategy

1. 🔲 ⬤ **Direct** students to **Workbook** page 119.

Workbook page 119

ROUTINE · Decoding Multipart Words in Context

a. **Assign** student partners.

b. **Have** students read the passage to themselves and use the decoding-multipart-words strategy for two difficult or unknown words. If students don't find any difficult words, **tell** students to practice on any two multipart words they find.

c. **Ask** students to discuss with their partners what they did. **Monitor** students. **Guide** as needed.

d. **Ask** students what they did.

Lesson Wrap-Up

Conclude with a brief review of reading skills and strategies taught (use the SQ3R strategy and use an online dictionary).

Continued: Unit 9 ✦ Lesson 2 **193**

Teacher's Edition: Unit 9, Lesson 2

T11 — Word-Learning Strategies

Word

. . . .

Context-Clues Strategy

When you come across a word you don't know,

Step 1: Read the sentence containing the word.

Step 2: Look for a definition or for examples of the word in the sentence.

Step 3: Read before or after the sentence for a definition or for examples of the word.

Word Meaning from Context

Glossary Definition

Dictionary Definition

Online-Dictionary Definition

Transparency 11

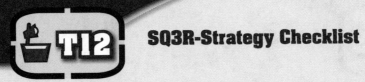

SQ3R-Strategy Checklist

	Yes
Survey	

Step 1: Make text connections.
    1: What's the topic of the lesson?
    2: What's your purpose for reading?
    3: What do you know about the topic?	

Step 2: Read the beginning of the lesson.	
Step 3: Look at the main part of the lesson.	
Step 4: Read the end of the lesson.	
Question	
One section at a time, change the lesson title, subheads, or bold and highlighted words into *who, what, where, when, why,* or *how* questions.	
Read	
One section at a time, read any question, and write the answer. Reread, and adjust reading rate as needed.	
Reflect	
Step 1: Reread your notes.	
Step 2: Think about how the topic relates to you, your world, and other things you've read.	
Review	
Step 1: Read the questions. Say the answers.	
Step 2: Read the answers. Say the questions.	

Note-Taking Form

Question (Page Number)	Answer

Transparency 13

Unit 9
Social Studies

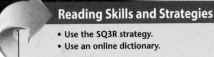

Reading Skills and Strategies
• Use the SQ3R strategy.
• Use an online dictionary.

Lesson 2 The Panama Canal

As YOU Read!

What You'll Learn
■ Why building the Panama Canal posed challenges
■ How the United States obtained control of the Panama Canal

Why It's Important
The story of the Panama Canal shows how economic and military considerations affect government decisions.

Key Terms
■ canal
■ lock

Everyone likes shortcuts. They save time and effort. As early as 1850, shipping companies and American presidents were pushing for a shortcut between the Atlantic and the Pacific Oceans.

Early Efforts

For years, any ship sailing from New York to San Francisco had to go around the tip of South America—a voyage of thirteen thousand miles. A **canal,** or artificial waterway, through Central America would eliminate 60 percent of the distance. The best locations for a canal were Nicaragua and Panama.

Every American president since Ulysses S. Grant considered building a canal through Central America. A canal would save businesses time and money, and it would help the military. Battleships had no quick route between the Atlantic and the Pacific. The navy would face critical delays if the United States ever fought a war on both oceans. However, the French, not the Americans, were the first to try building a canal.

Since 1821, Panama had been part of Colombia. In 1881, Colombia sold land in Panama to a French company for a canal. Once the work began, the builders faced many challenges. A mountain range stood in the way, and mud slides erased much of the workers' progress. Worst of all, tropical diseases, such as malaria and yellow fever, killed twenty-five thousand workers. After a few years, the company ran out of money, and the canal was left unfinished.

The United States Steps In

In early 1902, President Theodore Roosevelt asked the House of Representatives for $140 million to build a canal across Nicaragua. Instead, Congress approved funds to buy the land from the French company and complete the route through Panama. Roosevelt offered $10 million and an annual rent of $250,000 to Colombian officials for the right to build the canal. Colombia refused the offer.

Content Reader: Unit 9, Lesson 2

Roosevelt decided to support a rebellion in Panama. A rebellion is a violent action by a large group of people to change a country's government.

◄ Many Americans criticized Roosevelt's interference in Latin American affairs.

An agent of the French canal company gathered a small army of Panamanians. On November 3, 1903, this group took over Panama City and declared independence from Colombia. Two days later, an American warship reached the coast of Panama and sent four hundred marines ashore. Eight more American warships formed a blockade to keep out Colombian ships. Roosevelt recognized the rebels as the new leaders of Panama, and the rebels gave the United States the right to build and control a canal.

Overcoming Difficulties

Building the canal might have been impossible if tropical diseases had gone unchecked. Fortunately, doctors had recently discovered that mosquitoes spread malaria and yellow fever. Mosquitoes need swamps or other standing water to multiply. The canal company hired a crew to fill swamps, cover water containers, and kill mosquitoes. Even so, of the 5,609 people who died while building the canal, many were victims of disease.

About 45,000 workers, most of them from the Caribbean, dug the canal. In addition to digging, they built locks and a dam. The **locks** adjusted water levels to raise and lower ships. Locks were necessary because the canal went through mountains. A dam was necessary to construct a lake for ships to sail across to the other side of Panama. The canal took eight years to complete. The dream of a passageway between oceans was realized.

◄ The canal is roughly fifty miles long. A ship can cross it in about eight hours.

Lesson Assessment

Review

1. **Explain** How would a canal help businesses and the military?

2. **Describe** How do locks help ships cross the Panama Canal?

3. **Summarize** What challenges did canal builders face?

4. **Conclude** Why did more workers die of tropical diseases during the canal project in the 1880s than during the project in the early twentieth century?

5. **Judge** Do you approve or disapprove of Roosevelt's support for the rebellion in Panama? Give reasons for your answer.

Critical Thinking

Why, do you think, did the French canal company organize the rebellion in Panama?

Writing in Social Studies

Write lyrics for a song about the Panama Canal to the tune of one of your favorite songs.

The Panama Canal **113**

Content Reader: Unit 9, Lesson 2

Lesson 2

SQ3R-Strategy Checklist

Name _____ Date _____

	Yes
Survey	

Step 1: Make text connections.
   1: What's the topic of the lesson?
   2: What's your purpose for reading?
   3: What do you know about the topic?	

Step 2: Read the beginning of the lesson.	
Step 3: Look at the main part of the lesson.	
Step 4: Read the end of the lesson.	
Question	
One section at a time, change the lesson title, subheads, or bold and highlighted words into *who, what, where, when, why,* or *how* questions.	
Read	
One section at a time, read any question, and write the answer. Reread, and adjust reading rate as needed.	
Reflect	
Step 1: Reread your notes.	
Step 2: Think about how the topic relates to you, your world, and other things you've read.	
Review	
Step 1: Read the questions. Say the answers.	
Step 2: Read the answers. Say the questions.	

116 Unit 9 ✦ Lesson 2 ✦ Activity 1 SQ3R-Strategy Checklist

Unit 9
Social Studies

Lesson 2

Activity 2

Note-Taking Form

Name ______________________ Date __________

Question (Page Number)	Answer

Unit 9 ✦ Lesson 2 ✦ Activity 2 Note-Taking Form 117

Workbook: Unit 9, Lesson 2

Unit 9
Social Studies

Activity 3

Lesson 2

Word-Learning Strategies

Name _____ Date _____

Word

— —

Context-Clues Strategy

When you come across a word you don't know,

Step 1: Read the sentence containing the word.

Step 2: Look for a definition or for examples of the word in the sentence.

Step 3: Read before or after the sentence for a definition or for examples of the word.

Word Meaning from Context

Glossary Definition

Dictionary Definition

Online-Dictionary Definition

Unit 9
Social Studies

Activity 4

Fluency Practice: Decoding Multipart Words

Name _____ Date _____

The Fall of the Berlin Wall

In May 1945, the Allied side is winning World War II. Soviet troops capture Berlin, the German capital, and soon after, the city is divided. The French, the British, and the Americans occupy the west side. The Soviets occupy the east.

Eight years later, the former allies are enemies. The Soviet Union controls Eastern Europe, including East Germany, and the puppet governments in these countries forbid their people to visit the West. The one exception is Berlin. East Berliners can still cross into West Berlin. West Berlin is an island of opportunity outside the German-run government in Communist-controlled East Germany. In contrast, East Berliners receive low wages and are subject to harsh laws passed in the Soviet Union. In June 1953, thousands of East Berliners protest in the streets. Soviet tanks push back the crowds, and forty people die.

Another eight years pass. East Berlin's Communist leaders erect a wall between East and West Berlin. Armed guards with dogs patrol the entire length, and East Berliners who try to go over or under the Berlin wall are shot.

Fast-forward to 1989. Hungary is breaking away from the Soviets. In September, the Hungarian government stops restricting East German travel. Thousands of East Germans go through Hungary to West Germany.

The Germans who stay behind hold weekly protests. On November 4, a million protesters turn out in East Berlin. In response, the hard-line Communists in the East German government step down.

The government announces that people are free to go in and out of East Berlin. At midnight on November 9, the first crowds of East Berliners pass through the wall's gates. West Berliners greet them with cheers and whistles and hand out German money. (East German marks are worthless outside East Germany.)

For weeks afterward, people arrive at the wall to pound it with hammers and picks. Whole chunks disappear, and later, some bricks turn up in sculptures in faraway cities such as Paris and New York. Today, all that remains are two rows of paving bricks that mark the location of the Berlin wall.

Strategy Steps

Step 1: Underline all the vowel sounds.

Step 2: Make a slash between the word parts so each part has one vowel sound.

Step 3: Go back to the beginning of the word, and read the parts in order.

Step 4: Read the whole word.

Word 1

Word 2

Unit 9 ✦ Lesson 2 ✦ Activity 4 Fluency Practice **119**

Workbook: Unit 9, Lesson 2

Unit 22, Lesson 4

By Unit 22, **Units 1–21** activities have already been taught and include the following skills and strategies:

- Lecture note taking
- Strategy Bookmark:
  - Comprehension strategies, including SQ3R strategy ("Survey," with integrated text connections; "Question"; "Read," with integrated comprehension monitoring and text structure; "Reflect"; "Review") and QHL strategy
  - Vocabulary strategies, including decoding-multipart-words strategy and word-learning strategies (context clues, glossary, dictionary, online dictionary)
- Oral and silent reading: fluency practice
- Think-pair-share strategy

- All skills taught in Units 1–20 (see above) are applied to the classroom science textbook.

Unit 22, Lesson 4, includes the following skills and strategies:

- All skills taught in Units 1–20 (see above) are applied to classroom science textbook.

Lesson 4 specifics across the **three instructional tracks** include the following:

Part A: Comprehension Strategies: Strategy Bookmark: Comprehension Strategies

- Working with partners to complete the SQ3R strategy using the Strategy Bookmark and notebook paper.
- Working with partners to complete the QHL strategy using the Strategy Bookmark and notebook paper.

Part B: Vocabulary Strategies: Strategy Bookmark: Vocabulary Strategies

- Working with partners to complete a word-learning-strategies activity using the Strategy Bookmark and notebook paper.

Part C: Fluency Strategies: Oral Reading and Information Learned

- Working with partners to complete an oral reading and writing activity on notebook paper.

Unit 22 · Lesson 4

Reading Skills and Strategies

- Review text connections, text structure, comprehension monitoring, SQ3R, QHL, Strategy Bookmark, and word-learning strategies.

PART A ⏱ 25 minutes | TEACHER SUPPORT: STRONG — MODERATE — STUDENT INDEPENDENCE

Comprehension Strategies

Activity Strategy Bookmark: Comprehension Strategies

1. **Direct** students to retrieve their green Strategy Bookmark from their science textbook.

Transparency 13

ROUTINE · Using the Strategy Bookmark: SQ3R Strategy

a. **Assign** student partners.

b. **Show** Transparency 13: Note-Taking Form (T13). **Provide** notebook paper to students. **Have** students set up the paper for SQ3R notes.

c. **Direct** students to the beginning of the textbook section. **Assign** the total number of pages to be read.

d. **Have** students refer to the Strategy Bookmark as they complete on their own all SQ3R steps, look for text structure, and then discuss with their partners. **Have** students continue the process until they finish the section. **Monitor** students. **Guide** as needed.

e. **Ask** students to describe how they completed the SQ3R strategy. **Accept** reasonable responses.

f. **Ask** students what they did. **Write** on T13 as needed. (When you have completed this activity, **retain** T13 with any written notes for the next activity.)

NOTE: Before this activity, have ready for each student an encyclopedia, another resource book, or an online search engine and a Web site that includes information on the textbook-section topic. If you are unable to provide each student with a computer, provide computer access to small groups of students.

ROUTINE · Using the Strategy Bookmark: QHL Strategy

a. **Have** students continue to work with their partners. **Provide** notebook paper to students.

b. **Provide** students with access to an online search engine, or pass out encyclopedias or other resource books. **Have** students refer to the QHL strategy on the green Strategy Bookmark as they complete on their own all three QHL questions and then discuss with their partners. **Show** T13 from the previous activity as needed. **Monitor** students. **Guide** as needed.

c. **Ask** students what they wrote. **Write** on T13 as needed.

PART B ⏱ 10 minutes | TEACHER SUPPORT: STRONG — MODERATE — STUDENT INDEPENDENCE

Vocabulary Strategies

Activity Strategy Bookmark: Vocabulary Strategies

NOTE: Select a vocabulary word from the textbook section. (The definition must appear in context.)

1. **Direct** students to the vocabulary-strategies section on the green Strategy Bookmark.

Transparency 18

a. **Have** students continue to work with their partners. **Provide** notebook paper to students.

b. **Have** available for students a dictionary or an online dictionary.

c. The word you're going to define is [say word].

d. **Show** Transparency 18: Notebook Paper (T18) as needed. **Have** students write the word. **Write** on T18 as needed.

e. **Have** students refer to the Strategy Bookmark as they find and write the definition. **Monitor** students. **Guide** as needed.

f. **Ask** students for the definition and where it was found. **Write** on T18 as needed. **Accept** reasonable responses. (When you have completed this activity, **retain** T18 with any written notes for the next activity.)

2. Direct students to place the Strategy Bookmark in the next section of the textbook.

PART C · 10 minutes · **TEACHER SUPPORT** STRONG · MODERATE · **STUDENT INDEPENDENCE**

Fluency Strategies

Activity ▸ Oral Reading and Information Learned

1. Direct students to the textbook fluency passage from Unit 22, Lesson 1.

ROUTINE · Taking Turns and Information Learned

a. **Assign** student partners. **Provide** notebook paper to students.

b. **Ask** students to read orally and to take turns. **Monitor** students. **Guide** as needed.

c. **Have** students write three things they've learned and then discuss them with their partners. **Monitor** students. **Guide** as needed.

d. **Ask** students to read their answers. **Show** T18 from the previous activity as needed. **Write** on T18 as needed.

2. Have students take home notes from Lessons 1–4. **Tell** students to study these for the Lesson 5 assessment.

Lesson Wrap-Up

Conclude lesson with a brief review of reading skills and strategies taught (review text connections, text structure, comprehension monitoring, SQ3R, QHL, Strategy Bookmark, and word-learning strategies).

SRA Read to Achieve: Comprehending Content-Area Text

Placement Test

Overview

We recommend this Placement Test for students who have experienced reading difficulties in the past (for example, students identified to receive special education services or students at risk for school failure). For students reading at or above grade level in grades 6–12, the Placement Test is optional. When in doubt about a student's performance, administer the Placement Test. It is designed to give rate, accuracy, and comprehension information about students' reading performance. You can use this information to identify students who will benefit from the **Read to Achieve** program or who might be better placed in a program for lower performers, such as *Corrective Reading Decoding*. In addition, the Placement Test information will allow you to evaluate progress in students' reading performance on completion of the program.

Preparation

You will administer the Placement Test individually. Each test will require approximately 5 to 10 minutes. Reproduce one copy of Appendix B pages 84–87 for each student and one copy for each tester. Obtain a timer, pencils, and a stopwatch or a watch with a second hand.

Administration

Select a quiet location to administer the Placement Test. Students who will be tested at a later time should not be allowed to see or hear other students being tested. When administering the test, sit across from the student. The student should not be able to see what you are writing on the form.

Fill out the top lines of the test form (student information). Keep this completed test form, and give the student a clean copy of the test.

Active student engagement is enhanced when teachers maintain a brisk pace while teaching.

Assessment Sequence

Step	Activity
1	**Distribute** Part I Science Fluency Passage.
2	**Have** the student read aloud Part I Science Fluency Passage while you time for one minute.
3	**Make** a slash (/) after the last word read at the end of one minute.
4	**Record** the number of words read and the number of errors.
5	**Have** the student continue reading the passage silently.
6	**Collect** Part I Science Fluency Passage.
7	**Distribute** Part II Science Comprehension Questions.
8	**Allow** the student three minutes to complete the questions.
9	**Collect** Part II Science Comprehension Questions.
10	**Calculate** correct words per minute (CWPM) and percent accuracy for Part I fluency passages. **Fill in** the calculations box on the fluency-passage form.
11	**Calculate** percent correct for Part II Science Comprehension Questions. **Fill in** the calculations box on the comprehension-questions form. If the student reads at least 100 words per minute with 90 percent accuracy and answers at least 80 percent of the questions correctly for Parts I and II, go to Step 13 below. If the student does not meet the criterion in rate, accuracy, or comprehension, proceed to Step 12.
12	**Repeat** Steps 1–11 for Part III Social Studies Fluency Passage and Part IV Social Studies Comprehension Questions. If the student reads at least 100 words per minute with 90 percent accuracy and answers at least 80 percent of the questions correctly for Parts III and IV, go to Step 13 below. If the student does not meet the criterion in rate, accuracy, or comprehension, administer the *Corrective Reading Decoding Placement Test*.
13	**Place** the student in *SRA Read to Achieve: Comprehending Content-Area Text*.

Parts I and III

Tell the student the following:

Read this passage aloud for one minute starting with the title. Follow along with your finger so you don't lose your place. After the timing, you'll finish reading the passage silently. You'll then answer some comprehension questions without looking back at the passage. Read carefully.

Begin timing as soon as the student begins reading the title of the passage.

Record each decoding error the student makes in oral reading as follows:

Error Type	Recording	Scoring
Omits word	Put **X** on omitted word.	Count as error.
Adds word	Put **X** between the two words to show where word was added.	Count as error.
Misidentifies word	Put **X** on misidentified word.	Count as error. However, do not count the same misidentified word as an error more than once. (For example, if the student misidentifies *international* three times, count only one error.)
Misidentifies proper noun or numeral	Do not mark if misidentified. However, put an **X** on omitted proper nouns or numerals.	Do not count misidentified words as errors. (For example, if the student misidentifies *Norgay* one or more times, do not count as an error; if the student identifies *29,035* incorrectly, do not count as an error.) Count omitted words as errors.
Does not identify word within three seconds	Tell student word, and mark **X** on word. If student can't identify a proper noun or a numeral within three seconds, tell student word, but do not mark **X** on word.	Count as error. Do not count as errors proper nouns and numerals that aren't identified in three seconds.
Sounds out word but not at normal speaking rate	Ask, What word? If student does not say word at normal speaking rate, mark **X** on word.	Count as error.
Self-corrects word	Do not mark.	Do not count as error.
Rereads word or phrase	Do not mark.	Do not count as error.
Skips line in passage	Immediately direct student to line.	Do not count as error.

Make a slash (/) after the last word read at the end of one minute. Record the total number of words read by the student and the total number of errors at the top of the filled-in test form. Have the student continue reading the entire passage silently. Calculate the correct words per minute and percent accuracy.

Parts II and IV

Collect the fluency passage, and tell the student the following:

Read each question carefully, and fill in the circle next to the correct answer. You have three minutes to complete the questions.

Do not help the student decode words or identify answers. Collect the comprehension questions when the student has finished or at the end of three minutes.

Part II Answer Key	Part IV Answer Key
1. C 2. A 3. B 4. D 5. B	1. D 2. C 3. A 4. B 5. C

Placement Schedule
for Students in Grades 6–12

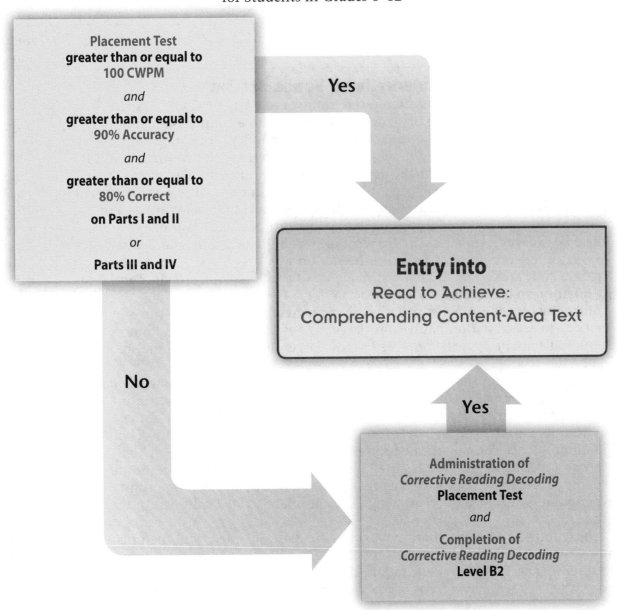

Placement Test
greater than or equal to 100 CWPM

and

greater than or equal to 90% Accuracy

and

greater than or equal to 80% Correct

on Parts I and II

or

Parts III and IV

Yes

Entry into
Read to Achieve:
Comprehending Content-Area Text

No

Yes

Administration of
Corrective Reading Decoding
Placement Test

and

Completion of
Corrective Reading Decoding
Level B2

Part I
Science Fluency Passage

Name _____ Class _____ Date _____

School _____ Tester _____

Calculations:

Number of Words Read _____   CWPM _____

– Number of Errors _____   ÷ Number of Words Read _____

CWPM = _____   % Accuracy = _____%

	Word Count
The International Space Station	4
In the past, some countries often raced against each other to explore space.	17
Now, many different nations are working together. These countries are building	28
the International Space Station (ISS). It is a space station all countries can use.	42
The United States, Russia, Canada, Japan, and several smaller countries built the	54
ISS together. The space station orbits more than two hundred miles above Earth.	67
Three crew members can live and work on the space station at the same time. The	83
nations take turns sending astronauts to the space station. At many times, crew	96
members from different countries work together on the space station.	106
The ISS was built in 1998. The first section was built and launched by Russia.	121
Several more pieces were added until the station was large enough for a crew.	135
The first crew arrived in 2000. It was made up of two Russian astronauts and one	151
astronaut from the United States.	156
Since the arrival of the first crew, other crew members have taken turns living in	171
the ISS. The space station has become larger as new crews visit and add more parts	187
to the station. The ISS will continue to grow larger until 2010. Then the station	202
will be full size.	206
What happens on the International Space Station? The crew members conduct	217
scientific experiments. One of the main experiments is being conducted on	228
the crew members themselves. This investigation explores how a weightless	238
environment affects humans over time. Scientists hope this information will help	249
in building space colonies in the future.	256
Some experiments involve testing how chemicals combine in space. Some	266
experiments explore the use of energy in space. One of the most important	279
experiments concentrates on growing plants in space to feed colonists in the	291
future.	292
The International Space Station will close in 2016. Scientists will then plan a	305
new space mission. What will that mission be? Perhaps it will involve living on	319
another planet. Would you like to join the crew?	328

Part II
Science Comprehension Questions

Name _____ Class _____ Date _____

School _____ Tester _____

```
Calculation:
    Number Correct        _____
  ÷ Number of Questions   _____5_____
    % Correct =           _____%
```

Fill in the circle next to the correct answer for each question based on what you just read.

1. Many different nations are working together to build the
   - ○ a. World Space Station.
   - ○ b. Global Space Station.
   - ○ c. International Space Station.
   - ○ d. Experimental Space Station.

2. The first crew arrived in 2000. It was made up of
   - ○ a. two Russian astronauts and one U.S. astronaut.
   - ○ b. four U.S. astronauts.
   - ○ c. one Japanese astronaut and one Russian astronaut.
   - ○ d. one Canadian astronaut and one Russian astronaut.

3. The space station orbits more than _____ miles above Earth.
   - ○ a. one thousand
   - ○ b. two hundred
   - ○ c. five thousand
   - ○ d. eleven thousand

4. In 2010, the space station will be full size. It will close in _____, and scientists will plan a new space mission.
   - ○ a. 2050
   - ○ b. 2025
   - ○ c. 2100
   - ○ d. 2016

5. Why do scientists conduct experiments on the space station?
   - ○ a. To understand how the atmosphere affects humans on Earth
   - ○ b. To help plan space colonies for the future
   - ○ c. To measure how other planets affect Earth
   - ○ d. To analyze how water evaporates on the moon

Part III
Social Studies Fluency Passage

Name _____ Class _____ Date _____

School _____ Tester _____

Calculations:

Number of Words Read _____

– Number of Errors _____

CWPM = _____

CWPM _____

÷ Number of Words Read _____

% Accuracy = _____%

	Word Count
At the Peak of Their Powers	6
Mount Everest is the highest point on Earth. Everest is part of the Himalaya	20
mountain range, which forms the border between the Asian countries of Nepal	32
and Tibet. In the 1950s, Mount Everest towered 29,028 feet above sea level. Today,	46
it measures 29,035 feet and is still rising. The plates under Asia's crust are always	61
shifting. They push Everest and the rest of the Himalayas about 1.6 to 3.9 inches	76
higher every year.	79
Between 1920 and 1952, seven mountain-climbing expeditions tried to	88
reach the top of Mount Everest. All failed. Europeans generally headed these	100
expeditions. They hired Sherpas—the local mountain-dwelling people—as guides	110
and porters. A nineteen-year-old Sherpa named Tenzing Norgay began going on	121
expeditions in 1935. By 1953, Norgay had been on six Everest expeditions. Not	134
one ever reached the top.	139
Thousands of miles to the south, Edmund Hillary was making a living as	152
a beekeeper. However, his passion was mountain climbing. He started in the	164
mountains of his native New Zealand. Eventually, he tackled the Himalayas. He	176
scaled eleven Himalayan peaks that towered 20,000 feet above sea level. His dream	189
was to conquer Mount Everest. In 1953, the Alpine Club of Great Britain invited	203
Hillary to join them on a climb to the top of Everest. Norgay was a member of the	221
expedition.	222
As the team members ascended, the oxygen in the air decreased. The air also	236
grew colder. The higher the team climbed, the more difficulty they had breathing.	249
To condition their lungs, they went up only 1,000 feet each day for several	263
days. Each night, they descended to camp. Still, climbing in the thin, frigid air	277
exhausted the men.	280
Around 26,000 feet, most of the team gave up. The only ones determined enough	294
to continue were Hillary and Norgay. On May 29, 1953, they became the first	308
climbers to reach the top of Mount Everest. Great Britain's Queen Elizabeth rewarded	321
Hillary by making him a knight. Norgay became a major celebrity across Asia.	334

Part IV
Social Studies Comprehension Questions

Name _____ Class _____ Date _____

School _____ Tester _____

Calculation:

Number Correct _____

÷ Number of Questions _____5_____

% Correct = _____%

Fill in the circle next to the correct answer for each question based on what you just read.

1. Which statement below is <u>incorrect</u>?
   - ◯ a. Mount Everest is the highest point on Earth.
   - ◯ b. The highest point on Earth is part of the Himalaya mountain range.
   - ◯ c. The highest mountain continues to rise due to plate shifting under Asia's crust.
   - ◯ d. The highest peak on Earth is around 20,000 feet.

2. The first climbers to reach the top of the highest peak were
   - ◯ a. Messner and Byrd.
   - ◯ b. Scott and Perry.
   - ◯ c. Norgay and Hillary.
   - ◯ d. Everest and Kropp.

3. What is one role of a Sherpa on a climb?
   - ◯ a. To guide climbers up and down the mountain
   - ◯ b. To provide shelter and warmth to climbers
   - ◯ c. To attach to rocks for climber safety
   - ◯ d. To offer medical assistance to climbers

4. In what year did the climbers reach the top of the highest peak on Earth?
   - ◯ a. 1900
   - ◯ b. 1953
   - ◯ c. 1975
   - ◯ d. 1961

5. Why did the climbers climb 1,000 feet each day and then descend to camp?
   - ◯ a. To have a warm bed to sleep in
   - ◯ b. To strengthen their legs
   - ◯ c. To condition their lungs
   - ◯ d. To plan their next route

APPENDIX C

Training Materials

Read to Achieve Training: Sample Agenda

Time	Topics Covered
8–8:30 A.M.	Overview: Purpose, features, and materials
8:30–9:15 A.M.	Instructional sequence: Chart, program examples, content-area units
9:15–9:30 A.M.	Scope and sequence
9:30–10 A.M.	Research base
10–10:15 A.M.	Break
10:15 A.M.–noon	Teaching techniques
Noon–12:45 P.M.	Lunch
12:45–1:30 P.M.	Placement Test
1:30–2:30 P.M.	Lesson samples and practice
2:30–2:45 P.M.	Break
2:45–4:00 P.M.	Lesson samples and practice (continued)

PowerPoint Training Outline

Program Overview
- Purpose
- Features
- Materials

Instructional Sequence
- Instructional-Sequence Chart
- Program Examples
- Content-Area Units

Scope and Sequence
- Three Tracks

Research Base
- Comprehension Strategies
- Vocabulary Strategies
- Fluency Strategies
- Higher-Order Thinking Skills

Teaching Techniques
- Setup and Program Introduction
- Following Routines
- Group and Individual Response
- Corrections
- Mastery and Firming
- Pacing
- Student Motivation and Validation
- Behavior Management
- Differentiated Instruction
- Lesson Acceleration and Remediation
- Homework

Placement Test

Sample Lessons

Program Overview

- Purpose (see *Professional Development Guide* page 2)
  - Explicit reading for understanding (students in grades 6–12)
  - Focus on content-area text, including science and social studies
  - Focus on *access* versus *content*
    - Read textbooks/informational text more effectively
    - Take notes from textbooks and classroom lecture
    - Study from notes

2

Program Overview

- Features (see page 2)
  - Differentiated instruction
  - Three-tier reading model
  - Varied science and social studies topics arranged in units
  - 45–50-minute lessons
  - Cumulative skill development based on Lexiles
    - 700L–900L for Units 1–9; 800L–1000L for Units 7–12; and 900L–1100L for Units 13–20; read own textbooks in Units 21–25
  - Explicit instruction
  - Text-based, collaborative learning
  - Focus on reading to learn
  - Real-world skills and strategies
  - Formative assessment
  - Generalization

3

Program Overview

- Materials (see pages 4 and 5)
  - Teacher Materials
    - Teacher's Edition
    - Transparencies
    - Professional Development Guide
    - Assessment Masters
    - ePresentation CD-ROM
    - Teaching Tutor CD-ROM
    - Online ePlanner
  - Student Materials
    - Content Reader
    - Workbook

4

Instructional Sequence

- Instructional-Sequence Chart (see page 6)
  - Strong teacher support
  - Moderate teacher support
  - Student independence (two types)
    - Work with a partner.
    - Work on your own and then discuss with your partner.
  - Review
  - Evaluation
- Program Examples (see page 7)
- Content-Area Units
  - 70% science (Units 1, 2, 5–8, 11–14, 17–20)
  - 30% social studies (Units 3, 4, 9, 10, 15, 16)
  - Teacher-selected textbooks (Units 21–25)

5

Scope and Sequence

- Three Tracks (see page 16)
  - Comprehension Strategies
    - Text features
    - Text structure
    - Comprehension monitoring
    - 3Q3R strategy and QHL strategy
    - Textbook note taking and lecture note taking
    - Strategy Bookmark
  - Vocabulary Strategies
    - Decoding-multipart-words strategy
    - Word-learning strategies (context clues, glossary, dictionary, online dictionary)
    - Strategy Bookmark
  - Fluency Strategies
    - Oral and silent reading with comprehension activities

6

Research Base (see page 22)

- Reading needs to be taught beyond elementary school (with a focus on adolescent readers).
- About 70% of older readers need remediation; very few need help decoding; most need help in comprehension.
- Majority of adolescent readers have difficulties accessing content-area text.
- Content-area text is tough.
- Explicit instruction is needed (teacher modeling, guided practice, independent practice).

7

Research Base

- Comprehension Strategies: The ultimate goal of reading instruction
  - *Text features:* Comprehending parts of a textbook (e.g., glossary, index)
  - *Text connections:* Relating to what is being read
  - *Text structure:* How text is organized
  - *Comprehension monitoring:* Determining when you don't understand and fixing your understanding
  - *Questioning and mnemonic strategies: SQ3R* (Survey, Question, Read, Reflect, Review) and *QHL* (What Questions do I have? How will I find the answers? What did I Learn after finding the answers?)
  - *Lecture-note taking:* Taking two-column notes (main ideas on left side; details on right side)

8

Research Base

- Vocabulary Strategies:
  Closely tied to reading comprehension
  - *Decoding multipart words:* Use before determining word meaning; a flexible strategy to help break words into smaller parts without using formal syllabication
  - *Word-learning strategies:* Ways of accessing word meaning in an independent manner
    - *Context clues:* Defining words using surrounding words or sentences
    - *Reference aids:* Using glossary, dictionary, online dictionary

9

Research Base

- Fluency Strategies:
  Reading text quickly, accurately, and with expression (leads to better comprehension)
  - *Repeated reading:* Reading text multiple times with an emphasis on oral reading

10

Research Base

- Higher-Order Thinking Skills
  - *Bloom's Taxonomy (Revised):* Continuum of questions, including Remembering, Understanding, Applying, Analyzing, Evaluating, and Creating
  - *Graphic organizers:* Visual aids that show how ideas are connected or organized
  - *Metacognition:* Thinking about your thinking

11

Teaching Techniques

- Setup and Program Introduction (see page 31)
  - Whole class or small groups
  - Students sit at desks or tables
  - Additional materials needed: colored pens (blue and red), timing device, notebook paper, teacher-selected textbooks
  - Teach expectations: ACES
    - Attend to the teacher
    - Collaborate with your partner
    - Express yourself through thoughtful comments and questions
    - Show your best work

12

Teaching Techniques

- Following Routines (see page 32)
  - Contain suggested wording on what you should say and do
  - Contain suggested student responses
  - Make it easier for you to teach rather than plan and write lessons
  - Change over time, from focused, teacher-directed routines to more concise, student-directed

13

Sample Routine

14

Teaching Techniques

- Group and Individual Response (see page 33)
  - Signal the group to respond together.
    - Use voice inflection.
    - Say "everybody" at the end of the question. (What did you write for Question 1, everybody?)
    - Use audible signal, such as a snap.
  - Call on a student for an individual response.
    - Put the student's name at the end of the question (How did you use the decoding-multipart-words strategy, Shane?)

15

Sample Routines

16

Teaching Techniques

- Corrections (see page 34)

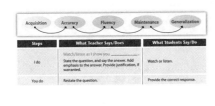

Steps	What Teacher Says/Does	What Students Say/Do
	Watch/listen as I show you . . .	
I do	State the question, and say the answer. Add emphasis to the answer. Provide justification, if warranted.	Watch or listen.
You do	Restate the question.	Provide the correct response.

17

Teaching Techniques

- Corrections ("Acquisition," "Accuracy")
  - If a mistake is made during group response:
    Use "I Do, You Do" with the entire group.
  - If a mistake is made during individual response:
    Use "I Do, You Do" with the entire group.
  - If you hear echoing during group response, or if a student isn't responding:
    Tell students you need to hear everyone together, and then repeat the question.

18

Teaching Techniques

- Corrections ("Fluency," "Maintenance," "Generalization")
  - Ask students if the answer is complete or correct.
  - Ask other students to raise their hands/thumbs when they hear an incorrect response.

19

Teaching Techniques

- Mastery and Firming (see page 36)
  - Mastery involves performing a skill or strategy until it is learned.
  - Mastery is enhanced through firming.
  - Firming is repeating a part of a routine that was troublesome.
  - When in doubt, repeat until firm.
  - *Read to Achieve* includes ample review to ensure mastery learning.
- Pacing (see page 36)
  - Use a brisk pace when teaching.
    - Covers more material
    - Increases student interest
    - Increases student achievement
    - Fewer behavior problems

20

Teaching Techniques

- Student Motivation and Validation (see page 37)
  - Success is motivating in and of itself.
  - Collaboration enhances student interest.
    - Students work with partners in most activities.
    - Think-pair-share activity is done every week.
  - Comment on students' success.
    - Say Yes, and repeat what the students did or said (e.g., Yes. You would use the Compare-and-Contrast Chart. . . .)

21

Teaching Techniques

- Behavior Management (see page 38)
  - Management issues can be seen as instructional opportunities.
    - *Here's what you're doing.*
    - *Here's what you need to do.*
    - Validate behavior when that behavior is shown.
  - Post expectations (ACES); Catch students being good.
  - Point systems: Add (don't take away) points.
  - Behavior contracts: Student and teacher agree and sign.
  - Self-management strategies (e.g., checklists, recording/monitoring forms)

22

Teaching Techniques

- Differentiated Instruction (see page 39)
  - Program structure allows you to teach more or less of the program.
  - Differentiated-instruction recommendations are aligned with assessment performance for students approaching mastery, students at mastery, and ELL students.
- Lesson Acceleration and Remediation (see page 39)
  - Units recommended for general-education students at or above grade level
  - Units recommended for general-education students at or below grade level
  - Units recommended for students in remedial reading or special education

23

Teaching Techniques

- Homework (see page 42)
  - Provide homework when students are independent in the use of a skill or strategy.
  - Do not assign homework if students are first learning a skill or strategy (strong or moderate teacher support).
  - Ideas
    - Mirror after "Beyond the Book" activities (appear in Content Reader and Teacher's Edition after Units 2, 4, 8, 10, 14, 16, and 20).
    - Follow differentiated-instruction charts, and assign activities.
    - Assign in-class activities that were not completed in class.
    - Allow students to practice newly learned skills and strategies in teacher-selected textbooks.

24

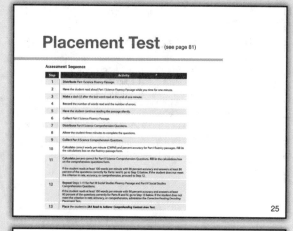

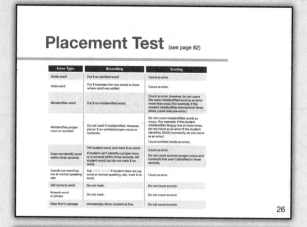

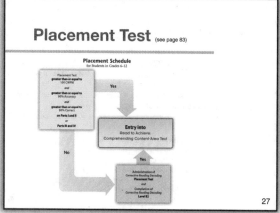

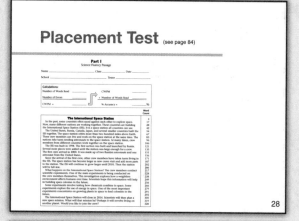

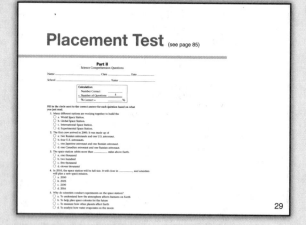

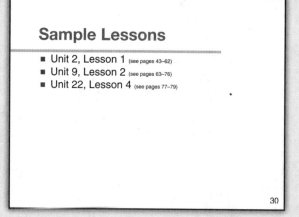